CRAFTS *and* ACTIVITIES
for WOMEN'S MINISTRY

Gospel Light

FOCUS ON THE FAMILY®

Gospel Light

Gospel Light is a Christian publisher dedicated to serving the local church. We believe God's vision for Gospel Light is to provide church leaders with biblical, user-friendly materials that will help them evangelize, disciple and minister to children, youth and families.

It is our prayer that this Gospel Light resource will help you discover biblical truth for your own life and help you minister to others. May God richly bless you.

For a free catalog of resources from Gospel Light, please call your Christian supplier or contact us at 1-800-4-GOSPEL or www.gospellight.com.

PUBLISHING STAFF
William T. Greig, Chairman · **Dr. Elmer L. Towns,** Senior Consulting Publisher · **Natalie Clark,** Product Line Manager · **Pam Weston,** Managing Editor · **Alex Field,** Associate Editor · **Jessie Minassian,** Editorial Assistant · **Bayard Taylor, M.Div.,** Senior Editor, Biblical and Theological Issues · **Rosanne Moreland,** Cover Designer · **Zelle Olson,** Internal Designer · **Carol Eide,** Contributing Writer

ISBN 0-8307-3367-1
© 2004 Focus on the Family
All rights reserved.
Printed in the U.S.A.

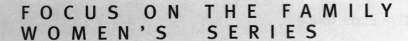

FOCUS ON THE FAMILY
WOMEN'S SERIES

The Purpose of the Focus on the Family Women's Series

And this is my prayer: that your love may abound more and more in know-
ledge and depth of insight, so that you may be able to discern what is best and
may be pure and blameless until the day of Christ, filled with the fruit of
righteousness that comes through Jesus Christ—to the glory and praise of God.
Philippians 1:9-11

The goal of this series is to help women identify who they are, based on their unique nature and in the light of God's Word. We hope that each woman who is touched by this series will understand her heavenly Father's unfathomable love for her and that her life has a divine purpose and value. This series also has a secondary goal: That as women pursue their relationship with God, they will also understand the importance of building relationships with other women to enrich their own lives and grow personally, as well as to help others understand their God-given worth and purpose.

The Purpose of Crafts and Activities for Women's Ministry

Women have an innate need to connect, build relationships and express themselves. Providing women with opportunities to be creative together and experience knowing each other through purposeful events and activities will allow them to build and deepen bonds of friendship, soften their hearts toward God and encourage growth in all areas of life.

Time is precious and women spend it carefully. Investing the hours and effort to make an event or activity memorable and significant will reap many benefits for all involved. When planning activities for the women, have a clear purpose in mind beyond filling a hole in the calendar.

Prayerfully consider how each activity will enable you to reach out and draw women in to a place where they feel welcome, accepted and special in God's sight. Understand the needs and interests of those you want to reach with a particular experience. Choose leaders, speakers and hostesses who can clearly communicate the purpose of the event or activity and who can represent Christ with integrity as they prepare for and serve the women. With these individuals in place, make the effort to create nothing but the best for them. This means praying for them, planning well and planning ahead.

PREPARING FOR CREATIVE EXPERIENCES

The keys to providing an effective ministry to women in your church and community include leadership, careful planning and attention to the interests and needs of the women whom you plan to serve, and attention to the technical requirements for the activities. This section contains the elements to help you plan the creative, fun elements of a complete women's ministry program.

chapter one

LEADERSHIP

Good leadership means making use of a variety of gifts and talents to get the job done right. Consider the following job descriptions as you prayerfully choose women God can use in these ways to comprise the core team of your women's ministry.

- **Coordinator**—An organizer with the ability to lead and delegate. This woman has a creative vision for fulfilling the needs and satisfying the interests of the women in your group and can direct the leadership team in its efforts.

- **Accountant/Treasurer**—A detail-oriented person who can track spending and monitor the budget. She is responsible for all financial paperwork and for coordinating finances with the buyer.

- **Buyer**—She is the ultimate bargain hunter. She is on every creative supplier's mailing list and loves to search the Internet, thrift shops and craft stores for creative ideas and great deals on resources. She has a good head for numbers, compares prices,

calculates quantities and stays within budget. A good relationship between the buyer, accountant/treasurer and coordinator is essential.

- **Project Designers**—This is in the plural because the best ideas are created when people dialogue with each other. These people can look at the available resources and the project ideas and make the project wonderful. They are creative, resourceful and thrifty!

- **Helping Hands**—Everything falls apart without these women. They assemble craft kits, set up and clean the work area and store supplies—they are the backbone of a positive creative experience.

- **Resource Helpers**—There are times when people with specific skills are needed. They can help you provide creative opportunities that reach beyond the skill level of the women in the ministry or the time constraints of your program. These helpers might cut wood to project specifications, sew items for the women to complete or teach new skills. Their help can make your creative activities even more special, and they can make more complex projects affordable. Developing resource helpers can be a great way to train future ministry leaders.

One person may fill more than one job position. In fact, overlap is healthy. Everyone on the team is a project designer and a helping hand. The struggle comes when one person tries to do everything. Her ability to serve will be short lived.

At least two to four members on the core team are ideal. Support and flexibility nourish creativity, make the work more effective and allow the team to serve with joy. Through communication and prayer, the team will find the balance that uses each person's gifts and talents for God's glory.

chapter two

PLANNING

One of the best ways to help your team function effectively and be wise stewards of your resources is to plan ahead.

1. Schedule a planning meeting two to three months before you begin your program year. This could be done as part of a Saturday leadership retreat or a morning or afternoon meeting specifically for planning creative activities.

2. Begin by purchasing a large calendar. Mark all holidays (including local school holidays) and any other regularly scheduled events that your church and community have planned. This will help avoid conflicts that might deplete attendance at meetings or events.

3. Schedule the meetings and events that will be part of your program, noting those meetings that will require special activities or crafts.

4. Keeping in mind your group's needs and interests, the budget and the available materials, plan the creative experiences you want to provide. Plan a few alternative creative activities or events that can be substituted or added, in case of changes in the schedule or in the needs of the group.

5. Calculate quantities of materials and make shopping lists.

6. Appoint leadership positions and delegate tasks to team members. Set deadlines for having materials purchased and prepared.

If possible, plan seasonal or holiday projects more than a year in advance. Craft stores often have items on sale immediately following a holiday season, so buying a year in advance can save a significant amount of money.

SHOPPING AND ACCOUNTING

The benefits of planning ahead are most obvious when you start shopping. You have time to look for the best sales, order materials from wholesale catalogs, comb through thrift stores and garage sales or gather discards from individuals. The pressure of time is minimized, the fun of the hunt is maximized, and the reward of being a good steward is gratifying.

The accountant/treasurer is in charge of tracking the spending, collecting receipts, taking care of financial paperwork and keeping the team posted about the great job the buyers are doing with spending. She can also compare the receipts against the shopping list to make sure no items are forgotten and report missing items or budget issues to the coordinator. Breaking the budget down by project will help the buyers stay on target.

To help defray the costs of a craft or activity, you could ask the women to donate a suggested dollar amount to help cover the cost of the activity in which they participate. This could also be done as a free-will offering.

You will be surprised at the money that can be saved by planning prudently. This extra money may even allow you to plan projects of greater quality. The women in your ministry will appreciate these above-and-beyond efforts.

The following page has a reproducible Shopping Worksheet to aid you. Complete one sheet for each project. Keep these sheets in a file or notebook for future planning reference. Writing notes and comments on the back of the sheet will also help in planning future projects or events.

SHOPPING WORKSHEET

Craft Title _____

Number of Craft Kits Needed _____ Date Materials Needed _____

Materials Needed	Quantity	Source	Cost
Total Cost			
Cost per Craft Kit			

chapter four

SUPPLIES

Now that the shopping has begun, where are you going to put all the materials? The ideal situation is to have a storage area near the women's meeting area. If a storage area is not available, ask the women in the women's ministry if someone has space in a garage, basement or a storage shed that can be used to store the craft materials.

It is prudent to consider security when storing the materials. The materials may walk off if others have easy access to them. If you cannot maintain a permanent storage area, invest in plastic storage bins that can be easily transported to and from the work area and that can be locked up when not in use. Some plastic storage bins have a place to add a small padlock to keep the items inside secure. Also consider ways to keep rodents and insects out of the supplies.

For the projects in this book, you will need to buy or have access to the following items:

❑ Photocopy machine and copier paper

❑ Kitchen and cooking utensils

❑ Sink

❑ Paper towels

❑ Cleaning supplies

❑ Iron(s) and ironing board(s)

❑ Sewing machine(s)

❑ Hot plate or electric frying pan/skillet

❑ Electrical outlets and heavy-gauge power cords*

Materials for specific projects should be kept together. In addition to these materials, you will also need to keep an ample stock of other basic supplies. The following page has a reproducible list of suggested supplies to keep on hand.

* **Note:** When several items are plugged into one electrical outlet at the same time, the flow of electricity diminishes. Be careful not to overload the electrical outlets. Also remember that the heavier the gauge of cord, the stronger the flow of power.

BASIC SUPPLIES

- ❑ Card stock in various colors
- ❑ Craft and fabric paints in various colors
- ❑ Disposable food-service gloves
- ❑ Duct tape
- ❑ Fine-point permanent-ink felt-tip pens in various colors
- ❑ Heavy-duty scissors for cutting cardboard or other heavy materials
- ❑ Heavy-gauge power cords
- ❑ Hole punches
- ❑ Hot-glue guns and hot-glue sticks
- ❑ Measuring sticks
- ❑ Metal pie pans (to hold hot-glue guns)
- ❑ Paper edgers
- ❑ Pencils
- ❑ Plastic tablecloths
- ❑ Power strips with multiple outlets
- ❑ Resealable sandwich bags
- ❑ Scissors for cutting fabric
- ❑ Scissors for cutting paper

- ❑ Small paint brushes
- ❑ Small sponge brushes
- ❑ White craft glue
- ❑ _____
- ❑ _____
- ❑ _____
- ❑ _____
- ❑ _____
- ❑ _____
- ❑ _____
- ❑ _____
- ❑ _____
- ❑ _____
- ❑ _____
- ❑ _____
- ❑ _____
- ❑ _____

chapter five

PREPARING CRAFT MATERIALS

Once all the materials have been purchased, the work of cutting and assembling the pieces for each craft begins. Depending on the project, you may want to create individual craft kits or simply provide precut or measured items in bulk.

This step in the preparation is where the adage "Many hands make light work" rings true. If you have been able to plan and purchase for several projects ahead of time—a season's worth is a good goal—you can organize a Preparation Night (or Afternoon) to get the work done. Preparation times can be a great way to get a tedious job done quickly and have fun too. It can also build teamwork and relationships within the craft and activity team.

This is where the resource helpers and helping hands listed in the leadership positions in chapter 1 can be of aid. Including those who will be teaching the crafts will help these leaders learn the crafts. You can also invite the women in your ministry to attend this event. Ask the helpers to bring the tools needed such as scissors, sewing machines, pins, etc. Provide a meal or at least dessert and beverages in appreciation for their efforts, and enjoy each other's company as you work. You will be amazed at how quickly fabric and ribbon are cut, beads or buttons are counted and friendships are built.

For individual kits, place all the small materials necessary for the kit in resealable bags. Oversized materials can be placed on a table with the bags of small materials during the craft or activity setup. Remember to include any needed instructions with each kit. Store specific items for each project with a list of basic supplies you will need for that particular project.

chapter six

TABLE SETUP SUGGESTIONS

There are several points to consider when arranging tables and seating for your creative experience. Technical considerations include space available and access to electrical outlets, a sink and the storage area.

The social aspect of table setup is of primary importance since the purpose of the experience is not only to create but also to interact with and encourage each other and to build friendships. The women will need adequate space to work, the freedom to move about and access to supplies as well as the opportunity to enjoy and learn from each other.

Working at round tables is good for interaction, but when using power cords, long tables arranged in a square or U-shape may work better. Leave openings between tables for women and helpers to circulate in order to access supplies and offer assistance.

One way to facilitate interaction (and often simplify your setup) is to get the women moving, rather than spending their entire activity time in one spot. Set up certain tasks in separate areas. For example, if glue guns are needed for a portion of the craft, set up a gluing station at one table. As the women share tools, materials and ideas, they will have an opportunity to support and encourage each other, thus building friendships.

Consider safety when setup includes electrical cords and hot-glue guns, electric skillets or irons. It might be necessary to tape cords to the floor to avoid tripping hazards.

TABLE SETUP CHART 1

For limited space and outlet access

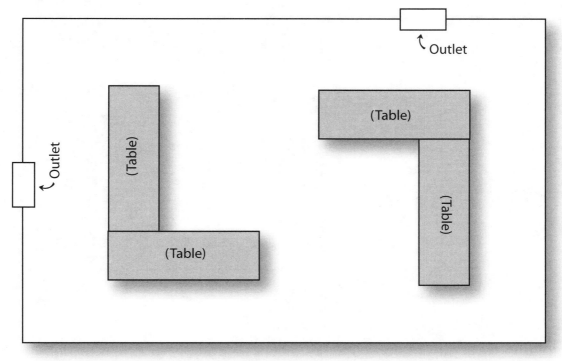

TABLE SETUP CHART 2

To facilitate interaction and simplify setup

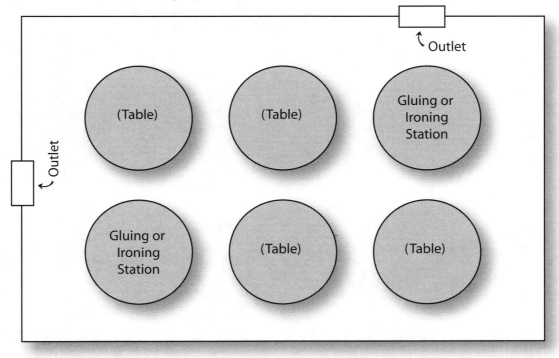

CRAFT IDEAS

These craft ideas have been divided into five groups: Fall, Winter, Spring, Summer and Anytime Crafts. Each craft idea features a page containing a complete materials list, preparation instructions, procedure information and sketches for the leadership team to use when planning the activity, shopping for materials, preparing materials and setting up the work area. In addition, there is a reproducible participant's page that can be photocopied and given to the women to help them complete the craft. Some craft ideas also provide reproducible masters for patterns or graphics required for the craft. See the Materials and Preparation section of each craft for planning details.

chapter seven

FALL

- Apple-Cinnamon Bread

- Funnel-Cake Mix

- Growth Chart

- Harvest Pumpkin

- Milk Money Bottle

- "My Child's Masterpiece" Wall Hanging

APPLE-CINNAMON BREAD

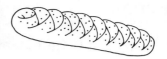

This delicious bread is a fall favorite! You can bake the completed breads together, or the women can take the unbaked bread home to enjoy fresh out of their own ovens. These tasty desserts can double as a service project if your group were to take them to a retirement community or use them as bake-sale items for your church's next youth group or missions event. The time required for the rising of the dough and for baking provides a great time to chat, play a relationship-building game (see chapter 19) or have your regularly scheduled meeting or Bible study!

Materials

For each person, you will need

- ❑ Photocopy of Apple-Cinnamon Bread Procedure Page

- ❑ ½ of a 1 lb. loaf of frozen bread dough, room temperature (follow the directions on the package for defrosting)

- ❑ 10 oz. of cinnamon-and-spice apple pie filling (about ½ of a can)

Additional Supplies

- ❑ Several small bowls

- ❑ Cinnamon and sugar (to sprinkle on top of each loaf)

- ❑ All-purpose flour

- ❑ Scissors for cutting paper

- ❑ Measuring stick

- ❑ Waxed paper

- ❑ Pencils

- ❑ Disposable food-service gloves

- ❑ Rolling pins (large wooden dowels—closet-rod size—cut in 12- to 18-inch lengths work well)

- ❑ Several pairs of clean kitchen scissors

- ❑ Vegetable oil spray

- ❑ Spoons

- ❑ Cookie sheets

- ❑ Aluminum foil, or French bread bags from local bakery supplier

- ❑ Plastic wrap

- ❑ Plastic bags for transporting baked loaves home

- ❑ Oven mitts

- ❑ Spatulas

- ❑ **Optional:** Cardboard and aluminum foil if transporting bread dough home for baking

Preparation

- Photocopy Apple-Cinnamon Bread Procedure Page for each person.

- Place cinnamon, sugar and flour in small bowls

Procedure

- Cut an 18-inch length of waxed paper and have each woman write her name on one end in pencil.

- Wearing food-service gloves, generously flour the waxed paper. On floured waxed paper roll dough into an 8x10-inch rectangle.

- Spoon a thin line of apple pie filling lengthwise down the center of the rectangle.

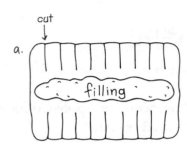

- Use scissors to make 2-inch cuts in dough, 1 inch apart, along long sides of the rectangle (see sketch a).

- Alternating sides, pull each cut strip over filling to give a braided look (see sketch b).

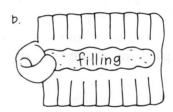

- Lightly spray the loaf with vegetable oil spray and sprinkle with cinnamon and sugar. Place on cookie sheet.

- **Optional:** To bake at home, place waxed paper with loaf on cardboard and loosely wrap with aluminum foil, making sure the foil does not stick to the dough. Place the covered loaf in a plastic bag for transporting it home.

- Let rise 15-25 minutes before baking.

- Preheat oven(s) to 350° F.

- Bake for 20-25 minutes or until golden brown. Let cool.

- Wrap cooled bread in foil or plastic wrap, or use French bread bags from a local bakery supplier.

Apple-Cinnamon Bread Procedure Page

A P P L E - C I N N A M O N   B R E A D

Procedure

- Cut an 18-inch length of waxed paper and write your name on one end in pencil.

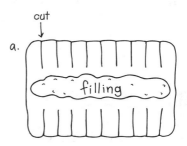

- Wearing food-service gloves, generously flour the waxed paper. On floured waxed paper roll dough into an 8x10-inch rectangle.

- Spoon a thin line of apple pie filling lengthwise down the center of the rectangle.

- Use scissors to make 2-inch cuts in dough, 1 inch apart, along long sides of the rectangle (see sketch a).

- Alternating sides, pull each cut strip over filling to give a braided look (see sketch b).

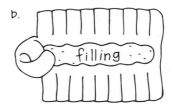

- Lightly spray the loaf with vegetable oil spray and sprinkle with cinnamon and sugar. Place on cookie sheet.

- **Optional:** To bake at home, place waxed paper with loaf on cardboard and loosely wrap with aluminum foil, making sure the foil does not stick to the dough. Place the covered loaf in a plastic bag for transporting it home.

- Let rise 15-25 minutes before baking.

- Preheat oven(s) to 350° F.

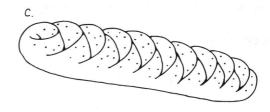

- Bake for 20-25 minutes or until golden brown. Let cool.

- Wrap cooled bread in foil or plastic wrap, or use French bread bags from a local bakery supplier.

FUNNEL-CAKE MIX

This craft doubles as a tasty treat! The packaging makes it an ideal gift for a neighbor, friend or family member, or the women may choose to make the funnel cakes themselves. This is another craft that could be used as a service project if your group were to take them to a new mother or use them as bake-sale or holiday-bazaar items for your church's next fund-raising project.

Materials

For each person, you will need

- ❑ Photocopy of Funnel-Cake Mix Procedure Page

For Mix

(These can be provided in bulk for women to measure out)

- ❑ 1 1/4 c. all-purpose flour
- ❑ 2 tbsp. nonfat dry milk
- ❑ 1 tbsp. granulated sugar
- ❑ 1 tsp. baking powder
- ❑ 1/8 tsp. salt
- ❑ Resealable sandwich-sized bag

For Bag

- ❑ Brown paper lunch bag
- ❑ 6 18-inch lengths of natural raffia
- ❑ Fabric for decoration
- ❑ 2 large buttons

- ❑ Rubber band
- ❑ Approximately 5-inch diameter plastic funnel in white or a harvest color
- ❑ Funnel Cake Recipe Master photocopied onto card stock

Additional Supplies

- ❑ Clean plastic bins
- ❑ Measuring cups and spoons
- ❑ Self-adhesive labels
- ❑ Fine-point permanent-ink felt-tip pens
- ❑ Disposable food-service gloves
- ❑ Scissors for cutting paper
- ❑ Scissors for cutting fabric
- ❑ Hot-glue guns and hot-glue sticks
- ❑ Hole punch
- ❑ Measuring stick

Preparation

- Photocopy the Funnel Cake Recipe Master onto colored card stock.

- Photocopy Funnel-Cake Mix Procedure Page for each person.

- Place each mix ingredient in a clean bin and provide the appropriate measuring utensil. **Note:** Ingredients do not need to be dumped into the bins; just place the product package in the bin so that the bin can catch spills.

- Label each bin with the quantity of the ingredient each mix requires.

- Place food-service gloves and resealable bags beside the bins.

- Cut raffia to specified length.

Procedure

For Mix

- Wearing disposable food-service gloves, measure mixed ingredients into sandwich bag as indicated and close securely.

For Bag

- Cut out facial features from fabric (carrot-shaped nose and round cheeks) using appropriate scissors. Glue features to the bottom half of the paper bag. Glue buttons to the bag for eyes, and use permanent markers to add stitching lines for mouth (see sketch a).

- Place plastic bag of mix in the paper bag.

- Fold raffia in half (reserve one piece of raffia for attaching recipe). Gather the top of the bag closed, adding fold of raffia. Wind rubber band around top of bag and raffia (see sketch b).

- Place funnel, narrow-end up, over top of paper bag. A touch of hot glue will hold funnel onto the bag.

- Cut out funnel-cake recipe, punch hole as indicated and tie with raffia to neck of funnel. Glue knot of raffia to funnel to secure (see sketch c).

Funnel-Cake Mix Procedure Page

Procedure

For Mix

- Wearing disposable food-service gloves, measure mixed ingredients into sandwich bag as indicated and close securely.

For Bag

- Cut out facial features from fabric (carrot-shaped nose and round cheeks) using appropriate scissors. Glue features to the bottom half of the paper bag. Glue buttons to the bag for eyes, and use permanent markers to add stitching lines for mouth (see sketch a).

- Place plastic bag of mix in the paper bag.

- Fold raffia in half (reserve one piece of raffia for attaching recipe). Gather the top of the bag closed, adding fold of raffia. Wind rubber band around top of bag and raffia (see sketch b).

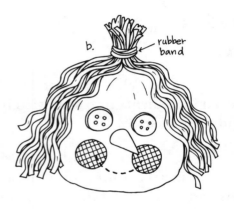

- Place funnel, narrow-end up, over top of paper bag. A touch of hot glue will hold funnel onto the bag.

- Cut out funnel-cake recipe, punch hole as indicated and tie with raffia to neck of funnel. Hot glue knot of raffia to funnel to secure (see sketch c).

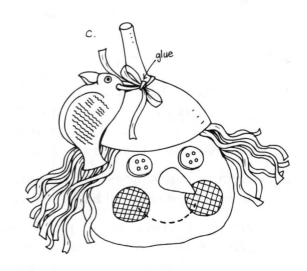

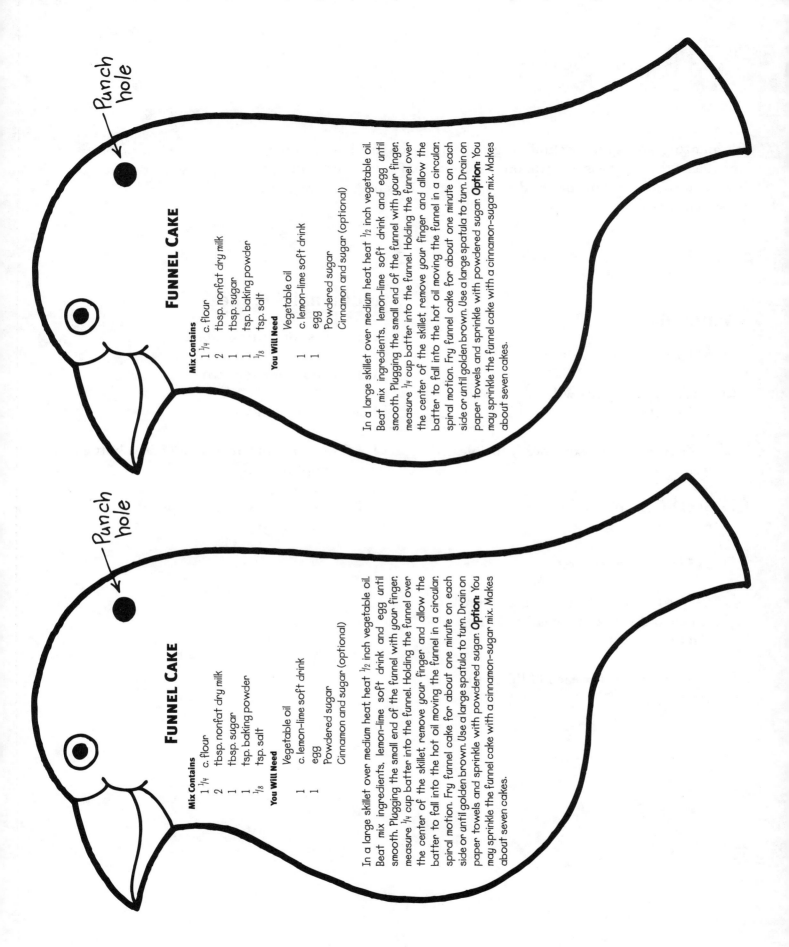

Punch hole

FUNNEL CAKE

Mix Contains

1 1/4 c. flour
2 tbsp. nonfat dry milk
1 tbsp. sugar
1 tsp. baking powder
1/8 tsp. salt

You Will Need

Vegetable oil
1 c. lemon-lime soft drink
1 egg
Powdered sugar
Cinnamon and sugar (optional)

In a large skillet over medium heat, heat 1/2 inch vegetable oil. Beat mix ingredients, lemon-lime soft drink and egg until smooth. Plugging the small end of the funnel with your finger, measure 1/4 cup batter into the funnel. Holding the funnel over the center of the skillet, remove your finger and allow the batter to fall into the hot oil moving the funnel in a circular, spiral motion. Fry funnel cake for about one minute on each side or until golden brown. Use a large spatula to turn. Drain on paper towels and sprinkle with powdered sugar. **Option:** You may sprinkle the funnel cake with a cinnamon-sugar mix. Makes about seven cakes.

Punch hole

FUNNEL CAKE

Mix Contains

1 1/4 c. flour
2 tbsp. nonfat dry milk
1 tbsp. sugar
1 tsp. baking powder
1/8 tsp. salt

You Will Need

Vegetable oil
1 c. lemon-lime soft drink
1 egg
Powdered sugar
Cinnamon and sugar (optional)

In a large skillet over medium heat, heat 1/2 inch vegetable oil. Beat mix ingredients, lemon-lime soft drink and egg until smooth. Plugging the small end of the funnel with your finger, measure 1/4 cup batter into the funnel. Holding the funnel over the center of the skillet, remove your finger and allow the batter to fall into the hot oil moving the funnel in a circular, spiral motion. Fry funnel cake for about one minute on each side or until golden brown. Use a large spatula to turn. Drain on paper towels and sprinkle with powdered sugar. **Option:** You may sprinkle the funnel cake with a cinnamon-sugar mix. Makes about seven cakes.

GROWTH CHART

It's amazing how quickly children grow! The Growth Chart will help document the progress as little ones sprout up. Parents and children love to keep a record of the children's changes. This makes a great gift for a new mom.

Materials

For each person, you will need

- ❑ Photocopy of Growth Chart Procedure Page

- ❑ 12-inch square of extra-heavy fusible web

- ❑ 36x12-inch strip of muslin, cut with pinking shears

- ❑ 5x5-inch square of felt

- ❑ 1/8 yard print fabric (a print from which individual shapes or figures can be cut out)

- ❑ One safety pin for each child in the family

Additional Supplies

- ❑ Scissors for cutting fabric

- ❑ Iron and ironing board

- ❑ Measuring sticks

- ❑ Fabric paint in various colors, in bottles with applicator tips

- ❑ Ballpoint pens or fine-point fabric-friendly felt-tip pens

Preparation

- Photocopy Growth Chart Procedure Page for each person.
- Cut fusible web, muslin and felt for each person to specified sizes.

Procedure

- Following manufacturer's instructions, apply fusible web to the back of the print fabric.
- Cut fabric into individual shapes or figures.
- Carefully trim around shapes and figures. Set aside one figure or shape for each child in your family. Arrange remaining shapes and figures to make a border across the top and bottom of muslin strip (see sketch a). Iron border in place, following manufacturer's instructions for the fusible web.
- Iron shapes of figures you set aside onto felt. Trim around each one leaving a small border of felt showing (see sketch b). Paint each child's name on a shape or figure.
- Use a measuring stick and pen to draw lines every inch along the left edge of the chart. Starting at the bottom, write a number to indicate every six inches beginning with 30 (2½ feet); then six lines up write 36, etc. (see sketch c).
- Use safety pins to attach felt-backed figures to the chart to indicate your children's heights (line the bottom of the figure up with your children's measurements). Move the figures up as your children grow. (Previous measurements and dates can be marked with a pen before moving figure.)
- Post the chart on a wall so that the bottom measurement is the corresponding distance from the floor.

Note: Do not wash the chart!

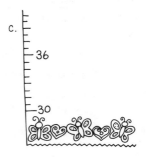

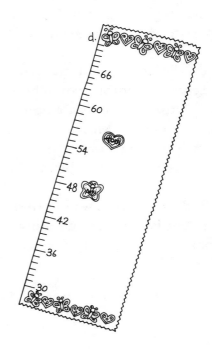

Growth Chart Procedure Page

Procedure

- Following manufacturer's instructions, apply fusible web to the back of the print fabric.

- Cut fabric into individual shapes or figures.

- Carefully trim around shapes and figures. Set aside one figure or shape for each child in your family. Arrange remaining shapes and figures to make a border across the top and bottom of muslin strip (see sketch a). Iron border in place, following manufacturer's instructions for the fusible web.

- Iron shapes of figures you set aside onto felt. Trim around each one leaving a small border of felt showing (see sketch b). Paint each child's name on a shape or figure.

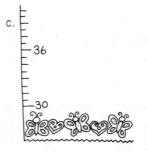

- Use a measuring stick to draw lines every inch along the left edge of the chart. Starting at the bottom, write a number to indicate every six inches beginning with 30 (2½ feet); then six lines up write 36, etc. (see sketch c).

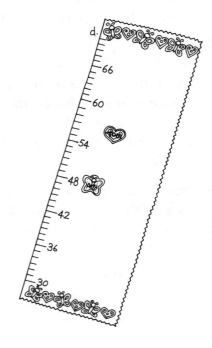

- Use safety pins to attach felt-backed figures to the chart to indicate your children's heights (line the bottom of the figure up with your children's measurements). Move the figures up as your children grow. (Previous measurements and dates can be marked with a pen before moving figure.)

- Post the chart on a wall so that the bottom measurement is the corresponding distance from the floor.

Note: Do not wash the chart!

28

HARVEST PUMPKIN

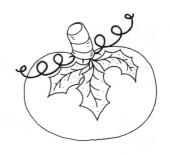

This cute decoration is ideal for the harvest season. Use it as a table decoration, as a gift or as an alternative to pumpkin carving.

Materials

For each person, you will need

- ❑ Photocopy of Harvest Pumpkin Procedure Page

- ❑ 22-inch diameter circle cut from harvest print or plain fabric

- ❑ 2x5-inch strip cut from green fabric

- ❑ Two 12-inch lengths of 20-gauge green floral wire

- ❑ ¹/₂ cup dry beans in a resealable bag

- ❑ Fiberfill (about the size of a volleyball when not compressed)

- ❑ Rubber band

- ❑ Small stem of silk ivy leaves (approximately 2 to 3 leaves)

Additional Supplies

- ❑ Measuring sticks

- ❑ Scissors for cutting fabric

- ❑ Wire cutters

- ❑ Pencils

- ❑ Masking tape

- ❑ Hot-glue gun and hot-glue sticks

Preparation

- Photocopy Harvest Pumpkin Procedure Page for each person.

- Cut fabric pieces and floral wire into specified sizes.

Procedure

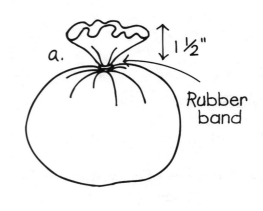

- Place the bag of beans in the center of the wrong side of the fabric circle. Place fiberfill over the bag. (The beans add weight to the bottom of the pumpkin, so it sits firmly.)

- Gather the edges of the fabric around the fiber-fill and wind a rubber band around gathered edges to make a 1½-inch stem (see sketch a).

- Wind the floral wire pieces around a pencil to shape tendrils. Tuck one end of each tendril under the rubber band on stem. Tuck stems of the ivy leaves under the rubber band as well (see sketch b).

- Tightly wrap the stem with masking tape to stiffen and hold tendrils and leaves in place.

- Fold the green fabric over the top of the stem and glue the end to the stem (see sketch c). Wind the folded green fabric around the stem, spot-gluing as needed, until it completely covers the masking tape and rubber band (see sketch d). Glue the end securely.

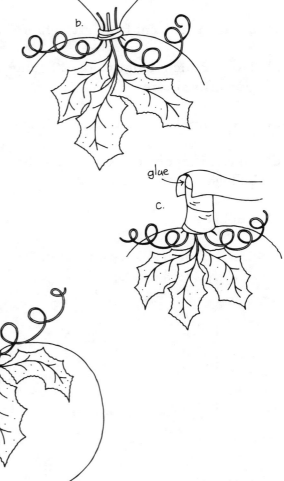

HARVEST PUMPKIN

Procedure

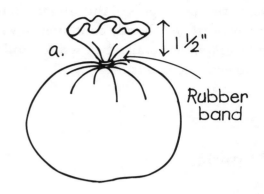

- Place the bag of beans in the center of the wrong side of the fabric circle. Place fiberfill over the bag. (The beans add weight to the bottom of the pumpkin, so it sits firmly.)

- Gather the edges of the fabric around the fiber-fill and wind a rubber band around gathered edges to make a 1 1/2-inch stem (see sketch a).

- Wind the floral wire pieces around a pencil to shape tendrils. Tuck one end of each tendril under the rubber band on stem. Tuck stems of the ivy leaves under the rubber band as well (see sketch b).

- Tightly wrap the stem with masking tape to stiffen and hold tendrils and leaves in place.

- Fold the green fabric over the top of the stem and glue the end to the stem (see sketch c). Wind the folded green fabric around the stem, spot-gluing as needed, until it completely covers the masking tape and rubber band (see sketch d). Glue the end securely.

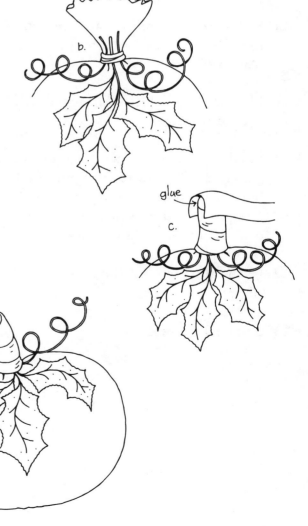

MILK MONEY BOTTLE

One of the harbingers of the fall season is that children (and adults) head back to school. The Milk Money Bottle is a handy container in which to collect change for children to use to buy lunch or beverages. It could also be used for collecting change for a particular missions project that your group elects to sponsor.

Materials

For each person, you will need

❑ Milk Label Master

❑ Self-adhesive mailing label measuring 1¹/₃ x 4 inches, 14 labels per sheet (Avery #5162)

❑ Photocopy of Milk Money Bottle Procedure Page

❑ Small jar or bottle with removable lid (glass Starbucks Frappuccino® bottles or plastic pint-sized Nestle Nesquik® bottles have a great shape, or use pint-sized canning jars)

❑ ¹/₂-inch wide x 2-foot length of ribbon

❑ Small silk flower

Additional Supplies

❑ Measuring stick

❑ Scissors for cutting fabric

❑ Fine-point permanent-ink felt-tip pens in various colors

❑ Hot-glue guns and hot-glue sticks

❑ **Optional:** craft paint in various colors and small paint brushes

Preparation

- Photocopy Milk Label onto mailing labels.

- **Optional:** Provide a photocopy of the label master as a reference for women to design and color their own label using felt-tip pens.

- Photocopy Milk Money Bottle Procedure Page for each person.

- Cut ribbon to specified length.

Procedure

- **Optional:** Use craft paint to add color to the jar lid. You may want to stipple various colors on the lid or paint a repeating pattern (e.g., dots, lines or shapes).

- Use felt-tip pens to add details and color to the label. **Optional:** Refer to the Milk Bottle Label Master and design a label of your own. Peel and stick label to the jar.

- Tie ribbon around the neck of the jar or bottle and make a bow. Glue the knot of the bow to the jar.

- Glue a small silk flower to the knot of the bow.

Milk Money Bottle Procedure Page

Procedure

- **Optional:** Use craft paint to add color to the jar lid. You may want to stipple various colors on the lid or paint a repeating pattern (e.g., dots, lines or shapes).

- Use felt-tip pens to add details and color to the label. **Optional:** Refer to the Milk Bottle Label Master and design a label of your own. Peel and stick label to the jar.

- Tie ribbon around the neck of the jar or bottle and make a bow. Glue the knot of the bow to the jar.

- Glue a small silk flower to the knot of the bow.

MILK MONEY BOTTLE

Procedure

- **Optional:** Use craft paint to add color to the jar lid. You may want to stipple various colors on the lid or paint a repeating pattern (e.g., dots, lines or shapes).

- Use felt-tip pens to add details and color to the label. **Optional:** Refer to the Milk Bottle Label Master and design a label of your own. Peel and stick label to the jar.

- Tie ribbon around the neck of the jar or bottle and make a bow. Glue the knot of the bow to the jar.

- Glue a small silk flower to the knot of the bow.

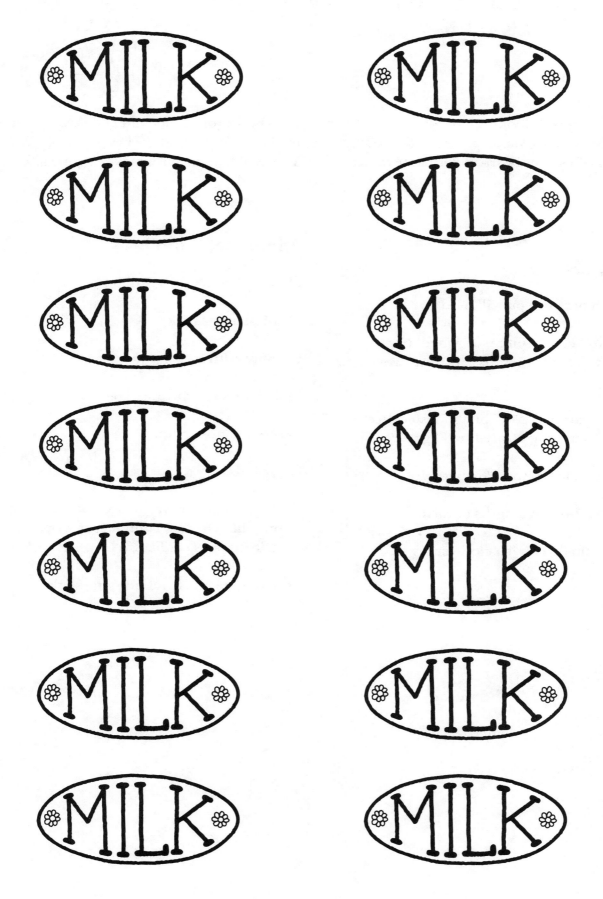

"MY CHILD'S MASTERPIECE" WALL HANGING

What mother isn't looking for new ways to display her child's (or grandchild's) creative masterpieces? "My Child's Masterpiece" Wall Hanging is an excellent way to show off her son's, daughter's or grandchild's handiwork in her home or her office. This wall hanging also makes a great gift.

Materials

For each person, you will need

- ❑ ¹/₂x6x12-inch piece of wood (weathered fencing scraps or pine works well)

- ❑ Photocopy of "My Child's Masterpiece" Wall Hanging Procedure Page

- ❑ 21-inch length of 18-gauge wire

- ❑ Three 24-inch lengths of raffia

- ❑ Two small wooden clothespins

Additional Supplies

- ❑ Drill and ¹/₈-inch drill bit

- ❑ Measuring stick

- ❑ Wire cutters

- ❑ Scissors for cutting paper

- ❑ Needle-nose pliers

- ❑ Pencils

- ❑ Craft paint in various colors and small brushes **Option:** Paint markers or colored felt-tip pens could also be used.

- ❑ Hot-glue guns and hot-glue sticks

Preparation

- Drill 2 ¹/₈-inch holes in wood that are 8 inches apart and ¹/₂ inch from one long edge.

- Photocopy "My Child's Masterpiece" Wall Hanging Procedure Page for each person.

- Cut wire and raffia to specified lengths.

Procedure

- Thread one end of the wire through one hole in the wood and twist the end around the wire to secure (see sketch a). Use pliers as needed. Repeat securing other end of wire through second hole in the wood.

- Bend and twist the length of the wire around a pencil or finger to add shape and dimension to it.

- Use craft paint and brushes to write "My Child's Masterpiece" on the wood (see sketch b).

- Glue two small clothespins 8 inches apart (opposite drilled holes) so that the clip part of the pin is pointing down off the bottom of the wood (see sketch b). Paint clothespins if desired. A child's artwork can be clipped to wall hanging and displayed.

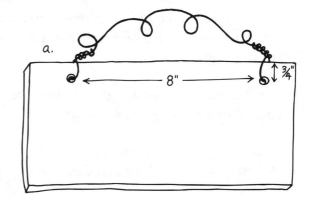

"MY CHILD'S MASTERPIECE"
WALL HANGING

Procedure

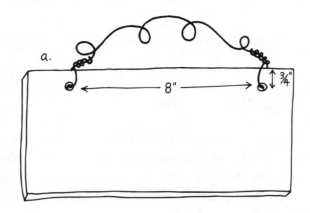

a. ←———— 8" ————→   ¾"

- Thread one end of the wire through one hole in the wood and twist the end around the wire to secure (see sketch a). Use pliers as needed. Repeat securing other end of wire through second hole in the wood.

- Bend and twist the length of the wire around a pencil or finger to add shape and dimension to it.

- Use craft paint and brushes to write "My Child's Masterpiece" on the wood (see sketch b).

- Glue two small clothespins 8 inches apart (opposite drilled holes) so that the clip part of the pin is pointing down off the bottom of the wood (see sketch b). Paint clothespins if desired. A child's artwork can be clipped to wall hanging and displayed.

- Tie three lengths of raffia into a bow around the wire to one side of the center.

b. My Child's Masterpiece

chapter eight

WINTER

- Christmas Lantern

- Gingerbread Gift Bag

- Mason Jar Votive

- New Year's Confetti Candle

- Pinecone Fire Starter

- Sweetheart Bookmark

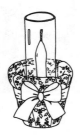

CHRISTMAS LANTERN

The classy design of the Christmas Lantern makes it ideal for dressy occasions as well as everyday use. Vary the look by choosing different colors of candles and ribbon. The Christmas Lantern also makes a great gift or a centerpiece for a Christmas party!

Materials

For each person, you will need

- ❑ Photocopy of Christmas Lantern Procedure Page

- ❑ 16-inch square of Christmas print fabric

- ❑ 4 feet of wide ribbon

- ❑ 5-inch-diameter terra-cotta pot

- ❑ 3 cups of sand

- ❑ Tall, clear-glass tumbler

- ❑ 8-inch taper or votive candle

Additional Supplies

- ❑ Scissors for cutting fabric

- ❑ Measuring stick

- ❑ Masking tape

- ❑ Hot-glue gun and hot-glue sticks

- ❑ Measuring cup

Preparation

- Photocopy Christmas Lantern Procedure Page for each person.

- Cut fabric and ribbon to specified lengths.

Procedure

- On the inside of the pot, cover the hole with masking tape.

- Place the pot in the center of the wrong side of the fabric square.

- Glue the center of each side of the square to the inside of the pot (see sketch a).

- Glue each corner of the square to the inside of the pot, neatly and evenly arranging the folds of fabric.

- Wrap the ribbon around the pot just below the rim and tie a bow. Glue the knot to the pot (see sketch b).

- Pour 1 cup of sand in the pot and 1 cup of sand in the tumbler. Place the tumbler in the center of the pot, open-end up, and add 3/4 to 1 cup of sand to the pot around the tumbler.

- Push the candle into the sand inside the tumbler.

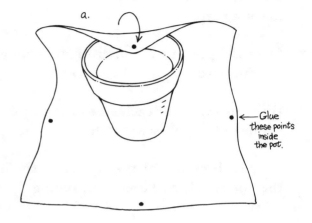

a.

Glue these points inside the pot.

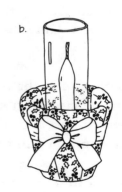

b.

CHRISTMAS LANTERN

Procedure

- On the inside of the pot, cover the hole with masking tape.

- Place the pot in the center of the wrong side of the fabric square.

- Glue the center of each side of the square to the inside of the pot (see sketch a).

- Glue each corner of the square to the inside of the pot, neatly and evenly arranging the folds of fabric.

- Wrap the ribbon around the pot just below the rim and tie a bow. Glue the knot to the pot (see sketch b).

- Pour 1 cup of sand in the pot and 1 cup of sand in the tumbler. Place the tumbler in the center of the pot, open-end up, and add ³/₄ to 1 cup of sand to the pot around the tumbler.

- Push the candle into the sand inside the tumbler.

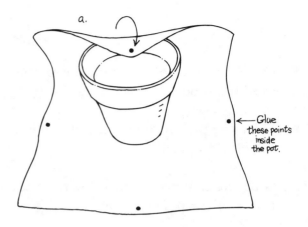

a.

Glue these points inside the pot.

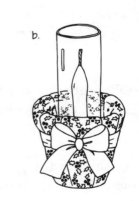

b.

GINGERBREAD GIFT BAG

Placing gifts in the Gingerbread Gift Bag is not only decorative but practical! The gift bag can be used as a Christmas decoration for years to come. Encourage the women to use their creativity to make each bag an original!

Materials

For each person, you will need

- ❑ Photocopy of Gingerbread Gift Bag Procedure Page

- ❑ 8-inch length of extra-heavy fusible web

- ❑ Christmas print fabric cut into a 1x9-inch strip and a 2x2-inch square

- ❑ Sheet of light brown felt

- ❑ Approximately 15-inch-long pre-sewn Christmas stocking or large white paper gift bag (do not use bags with a shiny finish)

- ❑ 4 small buttons or beads

- ❑ Scraps of Christmas trim and rick-rack

Additional Supplies

- ❑ Gingerbread Body Pattern

- ❑ Card stock

- ❑ Measuring stick

- ❑ Scissors for cutting fabric

- ❑ Scissors for cutting paper

- ❑ Pencils

- ❑ Iron and ironing board

- ❑ Hot-glue guns and hot-glue sticks

- ❑ Fabric paints in various colors

Preparation

- Photocopy Gingerbread Body Pattern onto card stock for each person.

- Photocopy Gingerbread Gift Bag Procedure Page for each person.

- Cut fusible web and Christmas print fabric into specified sizes.

Procedure

- Cut Gingerbread Body Pattern from card stock and trace two times on fusible web and two times on felt. Cut out bodies shaped from the fusible web.

- Follow manufacturer's instructions to apply fusible web shapes to the felt (inside outline traced on felt). Cut out body shapes from felt.

- Wrap the strip of Christmas print fabric around the neck of one shape to make a scarf for a boy; then arrange the two shapes on the bag (see sketch) and iron in place following manufacturer's instructions.

- Glue additional details to the bodies, using the Christmas-print-fabric square to make an apron for a girl, the buttons or beads for eyes, the fabric paint, trim and scraps for clothes, mouth, etc.

Gingerbread Body Pattern

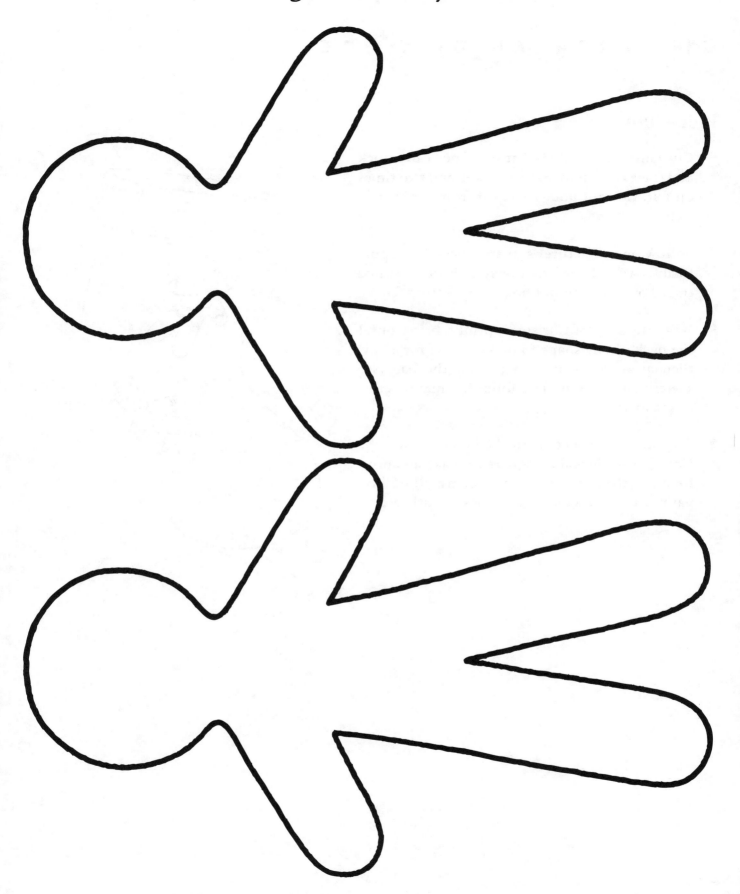

Gingerbread Gift Bag Procedure Page

GINGERBREAD GIFT BAG

Procedure

- Cut Gingerbread Body Pattern from card stock and trace two times on fusible web and two times on felt. Cut out bodies shaped from the fusible web.

- Follow manufacturer's instructions to apply fusible web shapes to the felt (inside outline traced on felt). Cut out body shapes from felt.

- Wrap the strip of Christmas print fabric around the neck of one shape to make a scarf for a boy; then arrange the two shapes on the bag (see sketch) and iron in place following manufacturer's instructions.

- Glue additional details to the bodies, using the Christmas-print-fabric square to make an apron for a girl, the buttons or beads for eyes, the fabric paint, trim and scraps for clothes, mouth, etc.

M A S O N   J A R   V O T I V E

The warm glow of the Mason Jar Votive will add warmth and a dramatic effect to long winter evenings. The contents of the jar can be varied to match a particular season or décor preference.

Materials

For each person, you will need

- ❏ Photocopy of Mason Jar Votive Procedure Page

- ❏ 24-inch length of ribbon to coordinate with colors of the filler for the jar

- ❏ 2 cups of filler for the jar: small ornaments, wrapped hard candies, nuts in their shells, silk flowers, potpourri, etc. **Note:** Be careful not to use highly flammable items.

- ❏ Pint-sized mason jar (not the wide-mouth version)

- ❏ Votive candle

- ❏ Round, clear-glass votive candle holder (it should be able to rest securely in the mouth of the mason jar, see sketch on next page).

Additional Supplies

- ❏ Scissors for cutting fabric

- ❏ Measuring stick

Preparation

- Photocopy Mason Jar Votive Procedure Page for each person.

- Cut ribbon to specified length.

Procedure

- Place filler in the jar.

- Place candle in the candleholder and set the holder in the mouth of the jar.

- Tie the ribbon around the mouth of the jar to form a bow.

- **Optional:** Use glass paint to decorate the outside of the jar.

M A S O N   J A R   V O T I V E

Procedure

- Place filler in the jar.

- Place candle in the candleholder and set the holder in the mouth of the jar.

- Tie the ribbon around the mouth of the jar to form a bow.

- **Optional:** Use glass paint to decorate the outside of the jar.

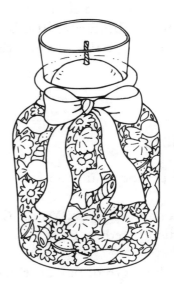

M A S O N   J A R   V O T I V E

Procedure

- Place filler in the jar.

- Place candle in the candleholder and set the holder in the mouth of the jar.

- Tie the ribbon around the mouth of the jar to form a bow.

- **Optional:** Use glass paint to decorate the outside of the jar.

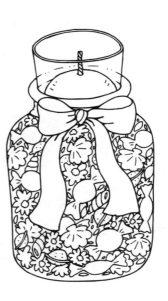

NEW YEAR'S CONFETTI CANDLE

What better way to celebrate the coming year than with the New Year's Confetti Candle? This celebratory craft is both festive and practical. Use brightly colored candles, ribbons and stickers to give these candles pizzazz!

Materials

For each person, you will need

- ❑ Photocopy of New Year's Confetti Candle Procedure Page

- ❑ 18-inch length of narrow ribbon

- ❑ 6 to 10 festive stickers

- ❑ 3-inch pillar candle

- ❑ 1 tsp. confetti

- ❑ Clear cellophane treat bag

Additional Supplies

- ❑ Scissors for cutting fabric

- ❑ Measuring sticks

Preparation

- Photocopy New Year's Confetti Candle Procedure Page for each person.

- Cut ribbon into specified length.

Procedure

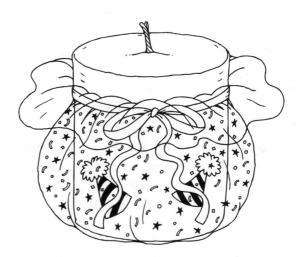

- Apply stickers to the candle.

- Place confetti in the clear treat bag.

- Place the candle in the bag.

- Tie the ribbon around the bag 1 inch from the top of the candle. Fold down the top edge of the bag over the ribbon if desired.

- Shake the bag to distribute the confetti.

Warning: Though pillar candles generally burn down the middle, be careful that the flame does not come near the cellophane treat bag or decorative stickers. You may wish to remove these items before burning the candle. Never leave a burning candle unattended.

NEW YEAR'S CONFETTI CANDLE

Procedure

- Apply stickers to the candle.

- Place confetti in the clear treat bag.

- Place the candle in the bag.

- Tie the ribbon around the bag 1 inch from the top of the candle. Fold down the top edge of the bag over the ribbon if desired.

- Shake the bag to distribute the confetti.

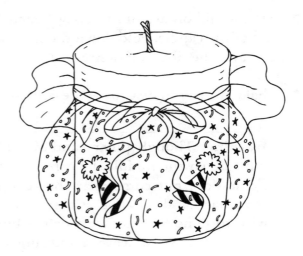

Warning: Though pillar candles generally burn down the middle, be careful that the flame does not come near the cellophane treat bag or decorative stickers. You may wish to remove these items before burning the candle. Never leave a burning candle unattended.

PINECONE FIRE STARTER

There's nothing like a crackling fire to make cold winter days cozy. The Pinecone Fire Starter is a decorative yet practical way to make starting those fires easier. It also adds a lovely scent to the air as you enjoy the cozy fire.

Materials

For each person, you will need

- ❑ Photocopy of Pinecone Fire Starter Procedure Page
- ❑ 12-inch length of cotton string
- ❑ 30-inch square of netting or tulle
- ❑ Three 24-inch-long pieces of raffia
- ❑ Large pinecone
- ❑ Heavy-duty paper plate

Additional Supplies

- ❑ Hot plate or electric skillet
- ❑ Paraffin wax
- ❑ Candle scent (about 1/4 block for every pound of paraffin)
- ❑ Number-10 steel can or large saucepan
- ❑ Wooden paint stick
- ❑ Tongs and old oven mittens
- ❑ Measuring sticks
- ❑ Scissors for cutting fabric

Preparation

- Photocopy Pinecone Fire Starter Procedure Page for each person.

- Heat hot plate or electric skillet to low. Melt paraffin and candle scent in the can or a saucepan on hot plate or in electric skillet, stirring once with a wooden paint stick when melted. Pan of wax should not be more than half full or it will overflow when pinecones are dipped. Paraffin is flammable, so do not leave it unattended.

- Cut cotton string, netting or tulle, and raffia to specified sizes.

Procedure

- Tie one end of string around the top petals of the pinecone.

- Holding the string, dip entire pinecone into the melted wax. Pull pinecone out of wax and hold above pot to allow excess wax to drop off before setting pinecone on a paper plate to cool.

- When wax on pinecones has cooled and hardened, trim the string to make a 2-inch wick.

- Gather tulle around the pinecone and tie with raffia.

Note: To use the Pinecone Fire Starter, unwrap the pinecone, place it in the fireplace, and then light the wick.

PINECONE FIRE STARTER

Procedure

- Tie one end of string around the top petals of the pinecone.

- Holding the string, dip entire pinecone into the melted wax. Pull pinecone out of wax and hold above pot to allow excess wax to drop off before setting pinecone on a paper plate to cool.

- When wax on pinecones has cooled and hardened, trim the string to make a 2-inch wick.

- Gather tulle around the pinecone and tie with raffia.

Note: To use the Pinecone Fire Starter, unwrap the pinecone, place it in the fireplace, and then light the wick.

SWEETHEART BOOKMARK

The Sweetheart Bookmark will remind women of their valentine all year! Or they can place a picture of themselves on the bookmark to give to their sweetheart, a parent, a sibling or a friend. With or without a picture, this practical valentine is sure to be a hit!

Materials

For each person, you will need

- ❑ Photocopy of Sweetheart Bookmark Procedure Page

- ❑ 3x9-inch strip of heavyweight colored art or scrapbook paper

- ❑ Two 3x4-inch pieces of coordinating paper

- ❑ Two 1-inch squares of magnetic sheeting (you can cut pieces from promotional magnets that vendors often provide to customers or purchase magnetic sheeting in craft stores)

Option: Ask women to bring a wallet-sized photo of their valentine to complete this craft, or they could add a photo later.

Additional Supplies

- ❑ Measuring stick

- ❑ Scissors for cutting paper

- ❑ Paper edgers, paper punches and/or corner croppers

- ❑ Glue sticks (the paste kind, not hot glue) or double-stick tape

- ❑ Fine-point permanent-ink felt-tip or gel pens

- ❑ Heavy-duty craft or flexible fabric glue

Preparation

- Photocopy Sweetheart Bookmark Procedure Page for each person.

- Cut paper and magnetic sheeting to specified sizes.

Procedure

- As desired, trim the edges and corners of long strip of paper using paper edgers, paper punches and/or corner croppers. Fold strip in half (see sketch a).

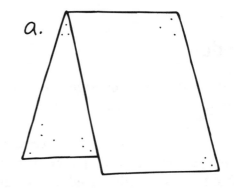

- Use edgers, punches and/or corner croppers to trim smaller pieces of paper into borders for a 1³/₄ x 2¹/₂-inch wallet-sized photo (different sized pieces may be layered behind the photo). Use glue sticks or tape to apply the borders to one half of the folded strip. Attach photo inside the paper border.

- Use felt-tip or gel pens to add words or details to the bookmark.

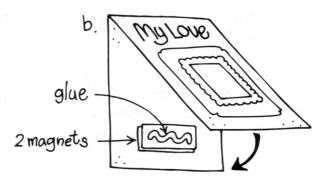

- Place two magnet pieces on top of each other so that they hold together. Use craft or fabric glue to attach magnets inside the folded halves of the bookmark (see sketch b). Let glue dry thoroughly before separating magnets.

> **Note:** To use finished bookmark, simply place the fold over the top of a page in a book. The magnets will hold the bookmark in place.

SWEETHEART BOOKMARK

Procedure

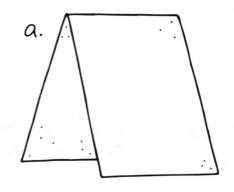

- As desired, trim the edges and corners of long strip of paper. Fold strip in half (see sketch a).

- Use edgers, punches and/or corner croppers to trim smaller pieces of paper into borders for a $1^3/_4$ x $2^1/_2$-inch wallet-sized photo (different sized pieces may be layered behind the photo). Use glue sticks or tape to apply the borders to one half of the folded strip. Attach photo inside the paper border.

- Use felt-tip or gel pens to add words or details to the bookmark.

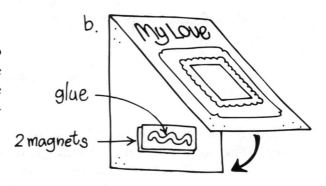

- Place two magnet pieces on top of each other so that they hold together. Use craft or fabric glue to attach magnets inside the folded halves of the bookmark (see sketch b). Let glue dry thoroughly before separating magnets.

Note: To use finished bookmark, simply place the fold over the top of a page in a book. The magnets will hold the bookmark in place.

chapter nine

SPRING

- Candy Greeting

- Garden Bell

- Garden Bunny

- Recipe Cards

- Scrumptious Cookie Mix

- Soap Gift

CANDY GREETING

What better way to say—well, just about anything!—than with chocolate? The Candy Greeting is sure to be a hit—not only with the women, but with the recipients as well! These could be made in bulk and given to shut-ins, youth or anyone else you want to encourage.

Materials

For each person, you will need

- ❑ Photocopy of Candy Greeting Procedure Page
- ❑ Candy bar with unprinted foil liner (gold or silver)
- ❑ Colored paper
- ❑ 3/4-inch sticker (a basic shape such as a heart or butterfly works best)

Additional Supplies

- ❑ Scissors for cutting paper
- ❑ Paper edgers
- ❑ Small paper punches
- ❑ Metallic gel pens

Preparation

- Photocopy Candy Greeting Procedure Page for each person.

- Using one original candy-bar wrapper as a pattern, cut colored paper so that it can wrap around the bar and the foil liner shows on each end.

Procedure

- Carefully slide the bar from its printed sleeve (do not remove the foil liner).

- Use paper edgers to trim the edges of the colored paper.

- Wrap the colored paper around the bar so that the ends meet in the back. Crease the paper along the edges of the bar; then remove the paper.

- Use paper punchers to punch various shapes on opposite sides of the section of wrapper that will cover the front of the bar.

- Use gel pens to write a word or phrase on the front section of the wrapper such as "Congratulations," "Thanks," or "I Love You."

- Wrap the paper around the bar and secure at the back with sticker.

CANDY GREETING

Procedure

- Carefully slide the bar from its printed sleeve (do not remove the foil liner).

- Use paper edgers to trim the edges of the colored paper.

- Wrap the colored paper around the bar so that the ends meet in the back. Crease the paper along the edges of the bar; then remove the paper.

- Use paper punchers to punch various shapes on opposite sides of the section of wrapper that will cover the front of the bar.

- Use gel pens to write a word or phrase on the front section of the wrapper such as "Congratulations," "Thanks," or "I Love You."

- Wrap the paper around the bar and secure at the back with sticker.

GARDEN BELL

In addition to its airy sound, the Garden Bell gives a decorative touch to any porch or garden. Encourage creativity as the women decorate the bells to suit their tastes.

Materials

For each person, you will need

❑ Photocopy of Garden Bell Procedure Page

❑ 1-yard piece and 6-inch piece of lightweight jute or rope

❑ 6-inch terra-cotta pot

❑ Round wooden clothespin

❑ Metal washer (outside of washer should be slightly larger than the hole in the bottom of the pot)

Additional Supplies

❑ Measuring stick

❑ Scissors for cutting fabric

❑ Acrylic craft paints in various colors

❑ Paint brushes in assorted sizes

❑ **Optional:** Clear acrylic spray sealer

Preparation

- Photocopy Garden Bell Procedure Page for each person.

- Cut lightweight jute or rope to specified lengths.

Procedure

- Use craft paint to apply a simple design to the pot: dots, hearts, stripes, flowers, spirals, etc. **Note:** Keep in mind that when Garden Bell is completed, the pot will be hanging upside down. Let dry.

- **Optional:** Once paint has dried, spray on acrylic sealer. Let dry.

- Fold 1-yard length of jute or rope in half. Slide the legs of the clothespin over the jute at the fold (see sketch a).

- Tie the 6-inch length of jute around the clothespin and long piece of jute at the neck of the clothespin (see sketch a). Trim excess.

- Knot together the two halves of the long piece of jute 3 inches above the head of the clothespin (see sketch b). Make sure knot is larger than the hole in the washer.

- Thread both ends of the long piece of jute through the hole in the washer and then up through the hole in the bottom of the pot (see sketch c).

- Knot together the ends of the jute (see sketch d).

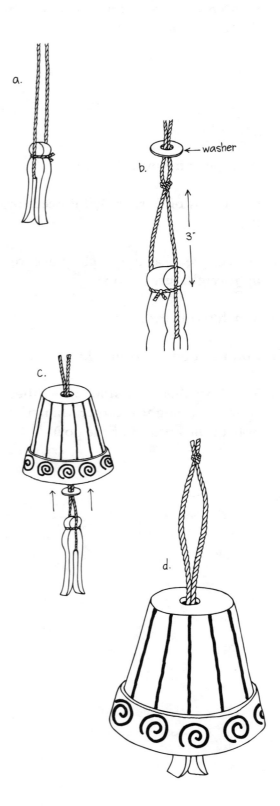

G A R D E N   B E L L

Procedure

- Use craft paint to apply a simple design to the pot: dots, hearts, stripes, flowers, spirals, etc. **Note:** Keep in mind that when Garden Bell is completed, the pot will be hanging upside down. Let dry.

- **Optional:** Once paint has dried, spray on acrylic sealer. Let dry.

- Fold 1-yard length of jute or rope in half. Slide the legs of the clothespin over the jute at the fold (see sketch a).

- Tie the 6-inch length of jute around the clothespin and long piece of jute at the neck of the clothespin (see sketch a). Trim excess.

- Knot together the two halves of the long piece of jute 3 inches above the head of the clothespin (see sketch b). Make sure knot is larger than the hole in the washer.

- Thread both ends of the long piece of jute through the hole in the washer and then up through the hole in the bottom of the pot (see sketch c).

- Knot together the ends of the jute (see sketch d).

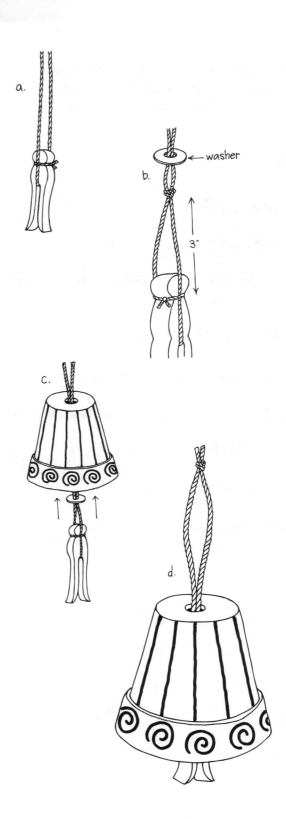

GARDEN BUNNY

The Garden Bunny is a great addition to a garden or potted plant. Simply push the wooden stick into the soil. Unlike your pets, this lovable animal doesn't need to be fed or cleaned up after!

Materials

For each person, you will need

- ❑ Photocopy of Garden Bunny Procedure Page

- ❑ Three 18-inch lengths of raffia

- ❑ Natural-colored cloth garden glove

- ❑ Fiberfill (enough to stuff glove)

- ❑ Wooden paint stick

- ❑ Small silk flowers

- ❑ Small straw hat

Additional Supplies

- ❑ Measuring stick

- ❑ Scissors for cutting paper

- ❑ Hot-glue gun and hot-glue sticks

- ❑ Pink and black fabric paint in bottles with applicator tip

Preparation

- Photocopy Garden Bunny Procedure Page for each person.

- Cut raffia to specified lengths.

Procedure

- Push the thumb of the glove inside out to form a pocket (see sketch a).

- Lightly stuff the glove with fiberfill.

- Insert the handle end of the paint stick into the wrist of the glove. Use raffia to securely tie the wrist closed around the stick.

- Bend the first and fourth fingers (pinky and pointer) down the sides of the front of the bunny (the side with the pocket) and glue to the body (see sketch a).

- Insert stems of silk flowers into the thumb pocket and glue them in place.

- Paint the tip of your own pinky finger with pink fabric paint, and then stamp the paint on the glove to make two cheeks for the bunny (see sketch b).

- Use black paint to make two dots for the eyes and a line for a smile from one cheek to the other (see sketch b).

- Cut a 3/4-inch circle from the top of the straw hat. Glue flowers to the hat. Slide the hat over one ear and down onto the bunny's head (see sketch b).

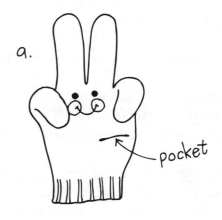

a.

pocket

b.

GARDEN BUNNY

Procedure

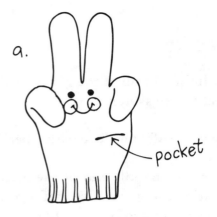

- Push the thumb of the glove inside out to form a pocket (see sketch a).

- Lightly stuff the glove with fiberfill.

- Insert the handle end of the paint stick into the wrist of the glove. Use raffia to securely tie the wrist closed around the stick.

- Bend the first and fourth fingers (pinky and pointer) down the sides of the front of the bunny (the side with the pocket) and glue to the body (see sketch a).

- Insert stems of silk flowers into the thumb pocket and glue them in place.

- Paint the tip of your own pinky finger with pink fabric paint, and then stamp the paint on the glove to make two cheeks for the bunny (see sketch b).

- Use black paint to make two dots for the eyes and a line for a smile from one cheek to the other (see sketch b).

- Cut a ³/₄-inch circle from the top of the straw hat. Glue flowers to the hat. Slide the hat over one ear and down onto the bunny's head (see sketch b).

RECIPE CARDS

With so many recipe books out there today, sometimes it's difficult to know which recipes to try. The Recipe Cards are a great way for women to share their favorite, tried-and-true recipes with each other. The gift pack of cards can be given away blank, or women can fill them in with their own recipes before giving them away. These would be a good gift for a new bride or to welcome new members to your group.

Materials

For each person, you will need

- ❑ Photocopy of Recipe Cards Procedure Page

- ❑ 3 sheets of card stock

- ❑ 12 stickers (of food, cooking, dishes, etc.)

- ❑ 1 yard of narrow ribbon

Additional Supplies

- ❑ Recipe Card Master

- ❑ Measuring stick

- ❑ Scissors for cutting fabric

- ❑ Scissors for cutting paper

- ❑ Colored pencils or markers

- ❑ **Optional:** food/dish stamps and stamp pad

Preparation

- Photocopy Recipe Cards Procedure Page for each person.

- Photocopy Recipe Card Master onto card stock.

- Cut ribbon to specified length.

Procedure

- Cut apart recipe cards as indicated. Fold each card in half.

- Use stickers and/or stamps to add detail to each card.

- Color border with colored pencils or markers.

- Stack the cards together and tie with ribbon for a gift (see sketch).

Recipe Cards Procedure Page

Procedure

- Cut apart recipe cards as indicated. Fold each card in half.

- Use stickers and/or stamps to add detail to each card.

- Color border with colored pencils or markers.

- Stack the cards together and tie with ribbon for a gift (see sketch).

Procedure

- Cut apart recipe cards as indicated. Fold each card in half.

- Use stickers and/or stamps to add detail to each card.

- Color border with colored pencils or markers.

- Stack the cards together and tie with ribbon for a gift (see sketch).

Recipe Card Master

Recipe For

Serves

Shared by

---- cut

Recipe For

Serves

Shared by

SCRUMPTIOUS COOKIE MIX

Women can give this delicious mix to a neighbor, friend or family member, or they can make the cookies for themselves. This activity is another opportunity to make the craft and share with new members and single parents or sell at a bake sale or holiday bazaar.

Materials

For each person, you will need

❑ Photocopy of Scrumptious Cookie Mix Procedure Page

❑ Five snack-sized resealable plastic bags

❑ Resealable sandwich bag

❑ Clear cellophane treat bag (approximately 5x10 inches pleated)

Ingredients for Each Mix

Have women scoop ½ c. of each of the following into separate snack-sized bags:

❑ Brown sugar (packed)

❑ Granulated white sugar

❑ Old-fashioned or quick oats

❑ Chocolate chips

❑ Coconut

Also

Have women scoop each of the following into the sandwich bag:

❑ 1½ c. flour

❑ ½ tsp. baking soda

❑ ½ tsp. salt

❑ ¼ tsp. baking powder

Additional Supplies

❑ Scrumptious Cookie Mix Label Master

❑ Clean plastic bins for ingredients

❑ Measuring cups and spoons

❑ Self-adhesive labels and a pen

❑ Disposable food-service gloves

❑ Colored card stock

❑ Staplers and staples

❑ Scissors for cutting paper or paper edgers

Preparation

- Photocopy the Scrumptious Cookie Mix Label Master onto colored card stock.

- Photocopy Scrumptious Cookie Mix Procedure Page for each person.

- Place each mix ingredient in a clean bin and provide the appropriate measuring utensil. **Note:** Ingredients do not need to be dumped into the bins; just place the product package in the bin so that the bin can catch spills.

- Label each bin with the quantity of the ingredient each mix requires. Group ingredients that go into snack-sized bags separately from the ingredients that go into the sandwich bag.

- Place food-service gloves and the appropriate resealable bags by the bins.

Procedure

- Wearing disposable food-service gloves, measure ingredients into resealable bags as indicated and seal securely. No air should be left in the bags.

- Layer bags of ingredients inside the treat bag. Fold down the top of the bag and staple it closed.

- Use scissors or paper edgers to trim the card-stock label. Fold the label in half.

- Place the fold of the label over the fold of the bag and staple the label in place (see sketch). Two staples, one at each bottom corner, work best.

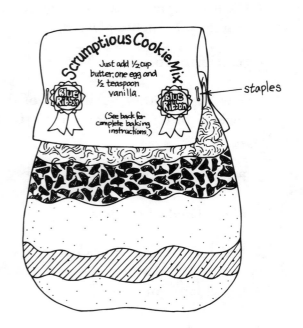

Note: See card-stock label for complete recipe and for baking instructions.

SCRUMPTIOUS COOKIE MIX

Procedure

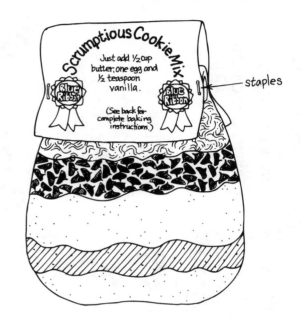

- Wearing disposable food-service gloves, measure ingredients into resealable bags as indicated and seal securely. No air should be left in the bags.

- Layer bags of ingredients inside the treat bag. Fold down the top of the bag and staple it closed.

- Use scissors or paper edgers to trim the card-stock label. Fold the label in half.

- Place the fold of the label over the fold of the bag and staple the label in place (see sketch). Two staples, one at each bottom corner, work best.

Note: See card-stock label for complete recipe and for baking instructions.

Scrumptious Cookie Mix Label Master

Fold

Scrumptious Cookie Mix

Just add ¹/₂ cup butter, 1 egg and ¹/₂ teaspoon vanilla.

(See back for complete baking instructions.)

Blue Ribbon

COCONUT CHOCOLATE-CHIP OATMEAL COOKIES

¹/₂ c. butter
¹/₂ c. brown sugar
¹/₂ c. granulated white sugar
1 egg
¹/₂ tsp. vanilla
    Flour mixture*
¹/₂ c. old-fashioned or quick oats
¹/₂ c. coconut
¹/₂ c. chocolate chips

Preheat oven to 300° F. Cream butter and sugars. Beat in egg and vanilla. Add flour mixture. Stir in oats; then add coconut and chocolate chips. Form 1-inch balls and place on ungreased cookie sheet. Bake 20 minutes or until lightly browned. Makes 30 cookies.
*Flour mixture contains 1 ¹/₂ c. flour, ¹/₂ tsp. baking soda, ¹/₂ tsp. salt, ¹/₄ tsp. baking powder

Cut

Scrumptious Cookie Mix

Just add ¹/₂ cup butter, 1 egg and ¹/₂ teaspoon vanilla.

(See back for complete baking instructions.)

Blue Ribbon

COCONUT CHOCOLATE-CHIP OATMEAL COOKIES

¹/₂ c. butter
¹/₂ c. brown sugar
¹/₂ c. granulated white sugar
1 egg
¹/₂ tsp. vanilla
    Flour mixture*
¹/₂ c. old-fashioned or quick oats
¹/₂ c. coconut
¹/₂ c. chocolate chips

Preheat oven to 300° F. Cream butter and sugars. Beat in egg and vanilla. Add flour mixture. Stir in oats; then add coconut and chocolate chips. Form 1-inch balls and place on ungreased cookie sheet. Bake 20 minutes or until lightly browned. Makes 30 cookies.
*Flour mixture contains 1 ¹/₂ c. flour, ¹/₂ tsp. baking soda, ¹/₂ tsp. salt, ¹/₄ tsp. baking powder

SOAP GIFT

This practical gift is ideal for all occasions. The type of soap you use will set the tone for the gift, so choose one that looks elegant and smells wonderful! Each woman could make several if enough supplies are provided. The possibilities for giving these gifts are limited only by each woman's imagination.

Materials

For each person, you will need

❑ Photocopy of Soap Gift Procedure Master

❑ 1½-inch-wide strip of wallpaper long enough to wrap around soap plus 1 inch

> **Note:** You can ask women to bring leftover wallpaper from their home-improvement projects or visit a wallpaper store and ask if you can have their discontinued books. Wallpaper can be used in a variety of crafts.

❑ Piece of raffia long enough to wrap around soap both ways and to tie a bow on top as on a gift (see sketch on next page).

❑ Bar of scented soap (handmade or glycerin soaps are nice)

❑ 1-inch square label or plain sticker

❑ Piece of clear cellophane large enough to wrap bar of soap

Additional Supplies

❑ Measuring stick

❑ Scissors for cutting paper

❑ Paper edgers

❑ Fine-point permanent-ink felt-tip pen

❑ Transparent tape

Preparation

- Photocopy Soap Gift Procedure Master for each person.

- Cut wallpaper and raffia to specified sizes.

Procedure

- If necessary, unwrap bar of soap.

- Use paper edgers to trim the long edges of the wallpaper strip.

- Wrap paper strip around the soap, overlapping ends, and tape together.

- Tie raffia around the soap in both directions and tie a bow on top (see sketch).

- With permanent pen, write a message, Bible verse reference or description of the soap on the label. Apply the label to the bottom of soap, securing the raffia to the paper.

- Use clear cellophane and tape to wrap the decorated bar of soap like a gift.

Procedure

- If necessary, unwrap bar of soap.

- Use paper edgers to trim the long edges of the wallpaper strip.

- Wrap paper strip around the soap, overlapping ends, and tape together.

- Tie raffia around the soap in both directions and tie a bow on top (see sketch).

- With permanent pen, write a message, Bible verse reference or description of the soap on the label. Apply the label to the bottom of soap, securing the raffia to the paper.

- Use clear cellophane and tape to wrap the decorated bar of soap like a gift.

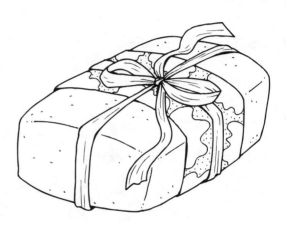

chapter ten

SUMMER

- Busy Bag

- Chili con Carne Mix

- Flannel Board

- Napkin Strap

- Patriotic Wind Chimes

BUSY BAG

The Busy Bag can be brought along whenever a child needs to be entertained, such as during a long car ride, while waiting for a doctor's appointment or when visiting a home where children are not present. Saving this bag for these special situations will make the contents of the bag more entertaining and special for the child.

Materials

For each person, you will need

- ❑ Photocopy of Busy Bag Procedure Page

- ❑ Photocopy of the Bag Contents Ideas Master

- ❑ Large natural-color tote bag, available at most craft or fabric stores

Additional Supplies

- ❑ Waxed paper

- ❑ Pinking shears

- ❑ Fabric scraps in colorful juvenile prints

- ❑ Scissors for cutting fabric

- ❑ Hot-glue gun and hot-glue sticks

- ❑ Fabric glue

- ❑ A variety of buttons and trims

- ❑ Fabric paints in various colors, in bottles with applicator tips

- ❑ **Optional:** fusible web, and irons and ironing boards

Preparation

- Photocopy Busy Bag Procedure Page for each person.

- Photocopy the Bag Contents Ideas Master for each person.

Procedure

- Place a layer of waxed paper inside the bag to keep the paint or glue from bleeding through.

- Use pinking shears to cut shapes from fabric scraps and to cut strips that can be used as borders or bows.

- Use hot glue or fabric glue to attach fabric shapes, trim, bows, buttons, etc. to one side of the bag. **Option:** Fusible web could also be used to attach accessories.

- Use fabric paint to add a child's name or message to the bag.

Busy Bag Procedure Page

B U S Y   B A G

Procedure

- Place a layer of waxed paper inside the bag to keep the paint or glue from bleeding through.

- Use pinking shears to cut shapes from fabric scraps and to cut strips that can be used as borders or bows.

- Use hot glue or fabric glue to attach fabric shapes, trim, bows, buttons, etc. to one side of the bag. **Option:** Fusible web could also be used to attach accessories.

- Use fabric paint to add a child's name or message to the bag.

Note: Fill the bag with age-appropriate toys and activities for children to enjoy during a long car ride, while waiting for a doctor's appointment or when visiting a home where children are not present, etc. Saving this bag for these special situations will make the contents of the bag more entertaining and special for the child.

Bag Contents Ideas

It is a good idea to switch items in and out of the bags to avoid boredom. On a long trip you might want to bring along a stash of items to switch out part way through the trip.

- Flannel board and felt shapes, letters or figures

- Small steel cookie sheet and magnets. **Note:** Pieces of magnetic strip can be glued to the back of dominoes or other game and puzzle pieces.

- Drawing materials and coloring books

- Beads and string, or sewing cards

- Small toys

- Finger puppets

- Edible treats in airtight containers

- Travel games

- Books

- Music and books on tape with a cassette player and headphones

- Maps

Note: Store everything in resealable bags. If you have a wide range of ages, use gallon-sized bags to store items for each age group.

CHILI CON CARNE MIX

There's no time like summer for a little south-of-the-border cuisine! This delicious Chili con Carne Mix is sure to be a hit with family and friends—and it is easy to fix on a busy day.

Materials

For each person, you will need

❑ Photocopy of Chili con Carne Mix Procedure Page

For Each Bag

❑ Chili con Carne Recipe Master photocopied onto colored card stock

❑ Fiesta-themed wrapping paper, cut to fit the front of the bag

❑ 12-inch length of yarn or brightly colored thin ribbon

❑ Lunch bag

For Each Mix

❑ Resealable snack-sized bag

❑ 2 c. dry pinto beans

❑ 2 cloves garlic

❑ 1 cube beef bouillon

❑ 1½ tsp. salt

❑ ½ tsp. oregano

❑ 1 tbsp. chili powder

Additional Supplies

❑ Measuring stick

❑ Scissors for cutting paper and/or paper edgers

❑ Scissors for cutting fabric

❑ Clean plastic bins

❑ Measuring cups and spoons

❑ Self-adhesive labels and a pen

❑ Disposable food-service gloves

❑ Craft glue

❑ Hole punch

Preparation

- Photocopy Chili con Carne Mix Procedure Page for each person.

- Photocopy the Chili con Carne Recipe Master onto colored card stock.

- Cut wrapping paper and yarn or ribbon to specified sizes.

- Place each mix ingredient in a clean bin and provide the appropriate measuring utensil. **Note:** Ingredients do not need to be dumped into the bins; just place the product package in the bin so that the bin can catch spills.

- Group the salt, oregano and chili powder bins together (they will be measured together into the resealable snack-sized bag).

- Label each bin with the quantity of the ingredient each mix requires.

- Place food-service gloves and resealable bags beside the bins.

Procedure

- Cover one side of the lunch bag with wrapping paper using craft glue.

- Use scissors or paper edgers to cut out recipe card. Fold card in half and punch holes in card as indicated on the recipe card.

- Measure beans and place beans, garlic and bouillon cube into lunch bag.

- Measure salt, oregano and chili powder into resealable snack-sized bag. Place snack-sized bag in lunch bag.

- Fold down top of lunch bag two times toward the wrapping paper side. Punch 2 holes, about 1/2-inch apart, at the center of the folded portion of the bag (see sketch a).

- Secure the recipe card to the bag by threading yarn or ribbon through the holes on the card and the bag and tying a bow. Recipe card and bow should be on the wrapping paper side of the bag (see sketch b).

Note: If giving the mix as a gift, write a personal note inside the recipe card.

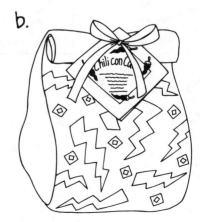

CHILI CON CARNE MIX

Procedure

- Cover one side of the lunch bag with wrapping paper using craft glue.

- Use scissors or paper edgers to cut out recipe card. Fold card in half and punch holes in card as indicated on the recipe card.

- Measure beans and place beans, garlic and bouillon cube into lunch bag.

- Measure salt, oregano and chili powder into resealable snack-sized bag. Place snack-sized bag in lunch bag.

- Fold down top of lunch bag two times toward the wrapping paper side. Punch 2 holes, about 1/2-inch apart, at the center of the folded portion of the bag (see sketch a).

- Secure the recipe card to the bag by threading yarn or ribbon through the holes on the card and the bag and tying a bow. Recipe card and bow should be on the wrapping paper side of the bag (see sketch b).

Note: If giving the mix as a gift, write a personal note inside the recipe card.

---

a.

b.

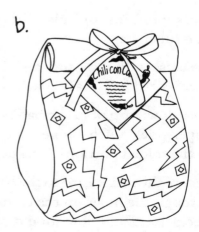

Chili con Carne Recipe Master

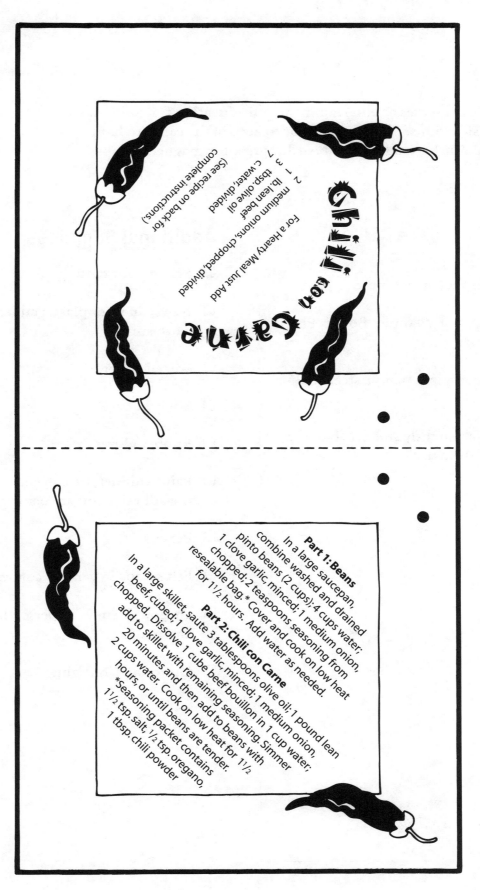

Chili con Carne

For a Hearty Meal Just Add
medium onions, chopped, divided
lb. lean beef
2 – 3 tbsp. olive oil
1 – 7 c. water, divided
(See recipe on back for complete instructions.)

Part 1: Beans
In a large saucepan, combine washed and drained pinto beans (2 cups); 4 cups water; 1 clove garlic, minced; 1 medium onion, chopped; 2 teaspoons seasoning from resealable bag. * Cover and cook on low heat for 1½ hours. Add water as needed.

Part 2: Chili con Carne
In a large skillet, saute 3 tablespoons olive oil; 1 pound lean beef, cubed; 1 clove garlic, minced; 1 medium onion, chopped. Dissolve 1 cube beef bouillon in 1 cup water; add to skillet with remaining seasoning. Simmer 20 minutes and then add to beans with 2 cups water. Cook on low heat for 1½ hours, or until beans are tender.
*Seasoning packet contains
1½ tsp. salt, ½ tsp. oregano,
1 tbsp. chili powder

FLANNEL BOARD

The Flannel Board serves as entertainment and education for children in a variety of situations. This is a great toy to keep in the car or to hang in a playroom. The backside of the board is great for magnetic shapes and games.

Materials

For each person, you will need

❑ Photocopy of Flannel Board Procedure Page

❑ Small metal pizza pan or steel cookie sheet

❑ Piece of felt slightly smaller than the inside of the pan

❑ Resealable sandwich bag

Additional Supplies

❑ Scissors for cutting fabric

❑ Newspapers or plastic tablecloths to cover work surface

❑ Waxed paper

❑ Spray adhesive

❑ Rubber gloves

❑ Paint thinner, or solvent appropriate for the adhesive you are using

❑ Pencils

❑ Felt scraps in various colors

❑ **Optional:** small paper or fabric pictures and magnets

❑ **Optional:** Craft glue

Preparation

- Photocopy Flannel Board Procedure Page for each person.

- Cut pieces of felt to be the same shape as the pan but slightly smaller.

- Cover tables with newspaper or plastic table-cloths and place in a well-ventilated area (out-doors if possible).

Procedure

- Lay the felt shape on a piece of waxed paper.

- On covered work surface, spray felt shape with spray adhesive—wear rubber gloves. Let dry for 1 to 2 minutes.

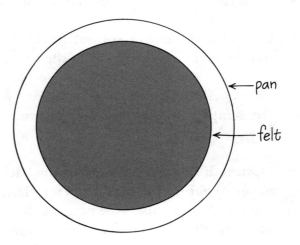

- Press the sticky side of the felt inside the pan.

- Use paint thinner or solvent to clean any adhesive from exposed surfaces of the pan.

- Use pencil to draw shapes, letters or figures onto felt scraps; cut out. Place shapes in a resealable bag.

- **Optional:** Felt can be glued to the back of small paper or fabric pictures to make flannel graph figures. You can also glue magnets to the back of pictures, Tic-Tac-Toe shapes or dominoes. These magnets can be used on the back of the steel pan. Store these items with the flannel board in a tote bag or backpack.

Note: If you are pregnant or have other health concerns, ask for assistance in applying adhesive.

FLANNEL BOARD

Procedure

- Lay the felt shape on a piece of waxed paper.

- On covered work surface, spray felt shape with spray adhesive—wear rubber gloves. Let dry for 1 to 2 minutes.

- Press the sticky side of the felt inside the pan.

- Use paint thinner or solvent to clean any adhesive from exposed surfaces of the pan.

- Use pencil to draw shapes, letters or figures onto felt scraps; cut out. Place shapes in a resealable bag.

- **Optional:** Felt can be glued to the back of small paper or fabric pictures to make flannel graph figures. You can also glue magnets to the back of pictures, Tic-Tac-Toe shapes or dominoes. These magnets can be used on the back of the steel pan. Store these items with the flannel board in a tote bag or backpack.

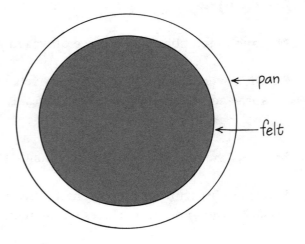

Note: If you are pregnant or have other health concerns, ask for assistance in applying adhesive.

NAPKIN STRAP

The Napkin Strap is a classy way to protect clothing from spills and messes. Depending on the materials you choose, this craft can be made for either an adult or a child to use.

Materials

For each person, you will need

❑ Photocopy of Napkin Strap Procedure Page

❑ 18-inch length of narrow ribbon

❑ 2 flat wooden shapes (butterflies, circles, apples, etc.) or large, flat decorative buttons

❑ 2 small (mini) wooden clothespins

❑ Cloth napkin or bandana

Additional Supplies

❑ Measuring stick

❑ Scissors for cutting fabric

❑ Craft paints in various colors and paint brushes (if using wooden shapes)

❑ Hot-glue gun and hot-glue sticks

❑ **Optional:** large-eyed needle

Preparation

• Photocopy Napkin Strap Procedure Page for each person.

• Cut ribbon to specified length.

Procedure

- Use craft paint to add details to one side of each wooden shape; let dry.

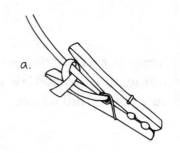

- Thread the ribbon through the center of the spring of one clothespin and securely knot the end around the spring (see sketch a). Repeat, tying the other end of the ribbon to the second clothespin. **Optional:** Use a large-eyed needle to thread ribbon through springs.

- Glue the wooden shapes or large buttons to the flat side of each clothespin (see sketch b).

Note: To use, place ribbon around the person's neck and clip the clothespins to the edge of a cloth napkin or bandana.

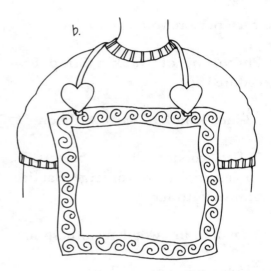

NAPKIN STRAP

Procedure

- Use craft paint to add details to one side of each wooden shape; let dry.

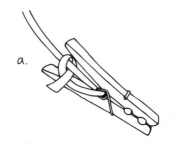

- Thread the ribbon through the center of the spring of one clothespin and securely knot the end around the spring (see sketch a). Repeat, tying the other end of the ribbon to the second clothespin. **Optional:** Use a large-eyed needle to thread ribbon through springs.

- Glue the wooden shapes or large buttons to the flat side of each clothespin (see sketch b).

Note: To use, place ribbon around the person's neck and clip the clothespins to the edge of a cloth napkin or bandana.

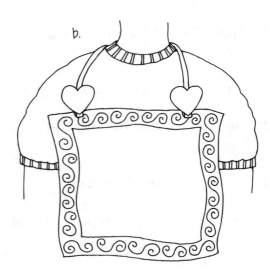

PATRIOTIC WIND CHIMES

The Patriotic Wind Chimes are visible and audible reminders of the blessings of freedom that we enjoy. **Note:** This craft can easily be modified to fit any season by altering the colors of paint.

Materials

For each person, you will need

❑ Photocopy of Patriotic Wind Chimes Procedure Page

❑ Three 18-inch lengths of lightweight jute

❑ 24-inch length of lightweight jute

❑ 1-foot-long piece of ¹/₄-inch-diameter dowel

❑ Three 2-inch terra-cotta pots

❑ Two 24-inch lengths of patriotic ribbon

Additional Supplies

❑ Measuring stick

❑ Scissors for cutting fabric

❑ Saw

❑ Small sponge brushes

❑ Craft paint in red, white and blue

❑ Small paint brushes

❑ Hot-glue gun and hot-glue sticks

❑ **Optional:** Gold or other accent color of craft paint

Preparation

- Photocopy Patriotic Wind Chimes Procedure Page for each person.

- Cut lightweight jute and ribbon to specified lengths.

- Cut dowels to specified length with saw.

Procedure

- Using sponge brush, paint the outside of each pot a different color.

- Paint details, stripes or patterns on pot (see sketch a).

- **Optional:** Use gold or other color to paint a message or symbolic words on each pot (e.g., "Life, Liberty, Happiness," "One Nation, Under, God"). Let dry.

- Tie a large knot at one end of each 18-inch length of jute. Thread the untied end of jute up through inside of each pot to make 3 bells (see sketch b).

- Tie each bell to the dowel, spacing evenly. If you want the bells to chime, they should all hang the same distance from the dowel.

- Tie the ends of the 24-inch length of jute to the ends of the dowel to make a hanger (see sketch c). Glue each knot of jute to the dowel to hold in place.

- Tie a length of ribbon into a bow on each end of dowel.

PATRIOTIC WIND CHIMES

Procedure

- Using sponge brush, paint the outside of each pot a different color.

- Paint details, stripes or patterns on pot (see sketch a).

- **Optional:** Use gold or other color to paint a message or symbolic words on each pot (e.g., "Life, Liberty, Happiness," "One Nation, Under, God"). Let dry.

- Tie a large knot at one end of each 18-inch length of jute. Thread the untied end of jute up through inside of each pot to make 3 bells (see sketch b).

- Tie each bell to the dowel, spacing evenly. If you want the bells to chime, they should all hang the same distance from the dowel.

- Tie the ends of the 24-inch length of jute to the ends of the dowel to make a hanger (see sketch c). Glue each knot of jute to the dowel to hold in place.

- Tie a length of ribbon into a bow on each end of dowel.

chapter eleven

ANYTIME CRAFTS

- Boo-Boo Bunny

- Drawer Sachet

- Garden Spot Centerpiece

- Herb Bath Pouch

- Homespun Note Cards

- Note Board

- Pasta Gift

- Western Soup

BOO-BOO BUNNY

Getting hurt is never fun, but the Boo-Boo Bunny can make cuts and scrapes more bearable for your little ones. These make great "bows" for baby shower gifts! Perhaps have the women make some for your church's nursery.

Materials

For each person, you will need

❑ Photocopy of Boo-Boo Bunny Procedure Page

❑ Large square lightweight washcloth

❑ 2 small rubber bands

Additional Supplies

❑ Rulers

❑ Black, white and pink fabric paint, in bottles with applicator tips

Preparation

- Photocopy Boo-Boo Bunny Procedure Page for each person.

Procedure

- Fold over 2 inches of two opposite sides of the washcloth (see sketch a).

- Fold up one unfolded edge until it is 3 inches below the opposite edge and wrap with a rubber band (see sketch b).

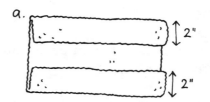

- Fold the remaining edge over the rubber band and pull down the corners to form ears. Wrap with a rubber band to form a head (see sketch c).

- Use fabric paint to make black and white eyes and a pink nose. Let dry.

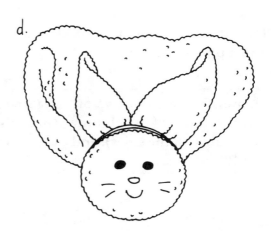

Note: To use, place two or three ice cubes in the body of the bunny (through the openings on the sides), and place it on the child's boo-boo.

Boo-Boo Bunny Procedure Page

Procedure

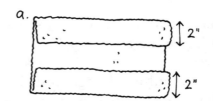

- Fold over 2 inches of two opposite sides of the washcloth (see sketch a).

- Fold up one unfolded edge until it is 3 inches below the opposite edge and wrap with a rubber band (see sketch b).

- Fold the remaining edge over the rubber band and pull down the corners to form ears. Wrap with a rubber band to form a head (see sketch c).

- Use fabric paint to make black and white eyes and a pink nose. Let dry.

> **Note:** To use, place two or three ice cubes in the body of the bunny (through the openings on the sides), and place it on the child's boo-boo.

DRAWER SACHET

This lovely Drawer Sachet will add a sweet scent to a drawer, linen closet or armoire. You may want to provide an assortment of fabric and ribbon for the women to choose from so that they can create something that suits their individual tastes. These sachets make nice gifts for visitors, shut-ins or those who are ill.

Materials

For each person, you will need

- ❑ Photocopy of Drawer Sachet Procedure Page

- ❑ 12-inch square of lace

- ❑ Two 18-inch lengths of ribbon

- ❑ 12-inch square of solid, silky fabric

- ❑ 1 to 2 tbsp. lavender or potpourri

- ❑ 8x10-inch piece of high-loft quilt batting

- ❑ 4 to 6 small silk flowers

Additional Supplies

- ❑ Measuring stick

- ❑ Scissors for cutting fabric

- ❑ Pinking shears

- ❑ Hot-glue gun and hot-glue sticks

Preparation

- Photocopy Drawer Sachet Procedure Page for each person.

- Cut lace and ribbon to specified sizes. Use pinking shears to cut silky fabric to specified size.

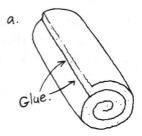

Procedure

- Glue lace to right side of silky fabric at the corners and side centers.

- Spread lavender or potpourri on batting. Roll the batting into 10-inch wide roll and glue long end to secure (see sketch a).

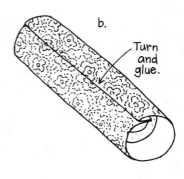

- Roll the lace covered fabric around fiberfill and glue edge to secure, turning under the raw edge of fabric before gluing (see sketch b).

- Tie ribbons to close each end of the fabric tube. Make a bow with ribbon; then glue silk flowers onto the knots of the bows. Trim ribbon if desired.

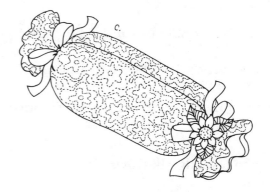

Procedure

- Glue lace to right side of silky fabric at the corners and side centers.

- Spread lavender or potpourri on batting. Roll the batting into 10-inch wide roll and glue long end to secure (see sketch a).

- Roll the lace covered fabric around fiberfill and glue edge to secure, turning under the raw edge of fabric before gluing (see sketch b).

- Tie ribbons to close each end of the fabric tube. Make a bow with ribbon; then glue silk flowers onto the knots of the bows. Trim ribbon if desired.

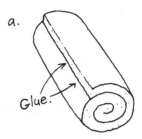

a.

Glue.

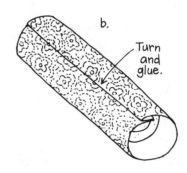

b.

Turn and glue.

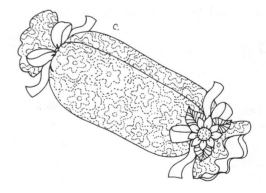

c.

GARDEN SPOT CENTERPIECE

The lovely Garden Spot Centerpiece brings a touch of the outdoors inside, no matter what the season!

Materials

For each person, you will need

- ❑ Photocopy of Garden Spot Centerpiece Procedure Page

- ❑ 5-inch terra-cotta pot

- ❑ 6x9-inch piece of foam board or wood

- ❑ 1/3 bag Spanish moss

- ❑ 3 small plastic speckled eggs

- ❑ Small artificial nesting bird

- ❑ 2 stems of silk flowers

Additional Supplies

- ❑ Thick garden gloves

- ❑ Safety glasses

- ❑ Resealable sandwich bag

- ❑ Hot-glue gun and hot-glue sticks

- ❑ Scissors for cutting paper

Preparation

- Photocopy Garden Spot Centerpiece Procedure Page for each person.

Procedure

- Wearing thick garden gloves and safety glasses, break open the bottom of the terra-cotta pot by turning it upside down over a hard object such as a piece of metal pipe, a chair leg or the end of a small dumbbell and tapping the bottom of the pot on the hard object (see sketch a). Place broken pieces in the sandwich bag and set aside.

- Place the broken pot on its side on the board and tack with hot glue.

- Glue a broken piece of the pot to board at each side of the pot, being sure to wedge the pieces under the pot to prevent the pot from rolling from side to side (see sketch b).

- Reserving a handful of moss, glue remaining moss to cover the board around the pot. Trim moss as needed. **Optional:** Glue small patches of moss on top of the pot.

- Glue remaining broken pot pieces around the pot and inside the pot by the broken bottom. **Note:** The pieces inside the pot will serve as a base for the nest and bird to rest against.

- Shape reserved moss into a small nest and glue nest inside pot.

- Glue eggs inside nest and bird to back edge of nest.

- Glue silk flowers around pot as desired.

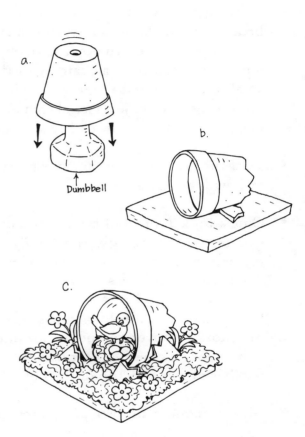

Garden Spot Centerpiece Procedure Page

GARDEN SPOT CENTERPIECE

Procedure

- Wearing thick garden gloves and safety glasses, break open the bottom of the terra-cotta pot by turning it upside down over a hard object such as a piece of metal pipe, a chair leg or the end of a small dumbbell and tapping the bottom of the pot on the hard object (see sketch a). Place broken pieces in the sandwich bag and set aside.

- Place the broken pot on its side on the board and tack with hot glue.

- Glue a broken piece of the pot to board at each side of the pot, being sure to wedge the pieces under the pot to prevent the pot from rolling from side to side (see sketch b).

- Reserving a handful of moss, glue remaining moss to cover the board around the pot. Trim moss as needed. **Optional:** Glue small patches of moss on top of the pot.

- Glue remaining broken pot pieces around the pot and inside the pot by the broken bottom. **Note:** The pieces inside the pot will serve as a base for the nest and bird to rest against.

- Shape reserved moss into a small nest and glue nest inside pot.

- Glue eggs inside nest and bird to back edge of nest.

- Glue silk flowers around pot as desired.

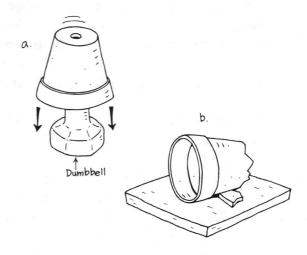

Dumbbell

HERB BATH POUCH

There are few things in life as relaxing as a hot bath. The Herb Bath Pouch creates a soothing, aromatic environment in which women can truly relax. Women can use the pouch themselves or give it as a gift.

Materials

For each person, you will need

- ❑ Photocopy of Herb Bath Pouch Procedure Page
- ❑ 6-inch square of lace
- ❑ 6-inch square or tulle or very fine netting
- ❑ 18-inch length of narrow ribbon
- ❑ Sprig of rosemary
- ❑ 1 heaping tbsp. dried lavender
- ❑ 1 level tbsp. chamomile
- ❑ Resealable sandwich bag
- ❑ Small rubber band

Additional Supplies

- ❑ Measuring stick
- ❑ Scissors for cutting fabric
- ❑ Plastic bins
- ❑ Measuring spoons
- ❑ Self-adhesive labels and a pen

Preparation

- Photocopy Herb Bath Pouch Procedure Page for each person.

- Cut lace, tulle or netting, and ribbon to specified sizes.

- Place herbs in bins with appropriate measuring spoons.

- Label each bin with the quantity of herb each pouch requires.

- Place resealable bags next to bins

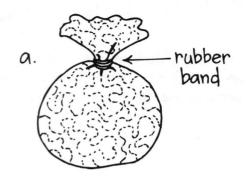

a.   rubber band

Procedure

- Remove the rosemary leaves from the stem and place the leaves in resealable bag.

- Add 1 heaping tablespoon lavender and 1 level tablespoon chamomile. Gently mix the contents of bag.

- Place lace down first, and then place tulle on top, matching edges.

- Pile herbs in the center of lace and tulle. Gather edges of lace and tulle around herbs and wrap with rubber band to close (see sketch a).

- Wrap center of ribbon around rubber band and knot securely. Tie a knot at the ends of the ribbon to form a large loop (see sketch b).

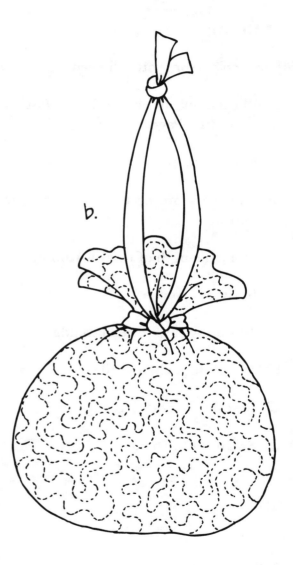

b.

Note: To use, hang the pouch so it is positioned under the tap of the bathtub. Fill the tub by running hot water over the pouch.

HERB BATH POUCH

Procedure

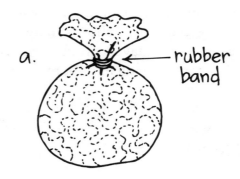

- Remove the rosemary leaves from the stem and place the leaves in resealable bag.

- Add 1 heaping tablespoon lavender and 1 level tablespoon chamomile. Gently mix the contents of bag.

- Place lace down first, and then place tulle on top, matching edges.

- Pile herbs in the center of lace and tulle. Gather edges of lace and tulle around herbs and wrap with rubber band to close (see sketch a).

- Wrap center of ribbon around rubber band and knot securely. Tie a knot at the ends of the ribbon to form a large loop (see sketch b).

Note: To use, hang the pouch so it is positioned under the tap of the bathtub. Fill the tub by running hot water over the pouch.

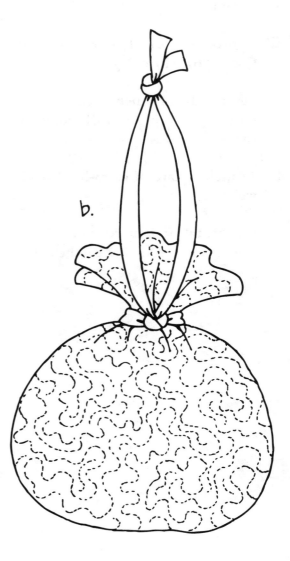

HOMESPUN NOTE CARDS

These handmade cards are a great way to send thoughtful messages year round. If you'd prefer, choose materials and fabrics that reflect a particular season or holiday, such as springtime or Christmas. This is another craft that can be made in bulk for gifts or to sell at bazaars.

Materials

For each person, you will need

- ❑ Photocopy of Homespun Note Cards Procedure Page

- ❑ Several 8½ x11-inch pieces of card stock (each piece will yield two cards)

- ❑ 12-inch square of extra-hold fusible web

- ❑ Cotton fabric that contains 6 to 10 figures or objects that can be cut out

Additional Supplies

- ❑ Measuring sticks

- ❑ Scissors for cutting fabric

- ❑ Scissors for cutting paper

- ❑ Irons and ironing boards

- ❑ Hot-glue guns and hot-glue sticks

- ❑ Scraps of cotton fabric, trim, ribbons and buttons

- ❑ Fine-point permanent-ink felt-tip pens

- ❑ **Optional:** paper cutter

Preparation

- Photocopy Homespun Note Cards Procedure Page for each person.

- **Option:** Use a paper cutter to cut card stock ahead of time.

- Cut fusible web to specified size.

Procedure

- Cut each piece of card stock in half to make two $5^1/_2$ x$8^1/_2$-inch strips. Fold each strip in half to make a card.

- Follow manufacturer's instructions to apply fusible web to the back of fabric. **Note:** Fusible web may also be applied to pieces cut from scraps of fabric, which make nice backgrounds or borders for print figures or objects.

- Cut out fabric figures or objects. Arrange on cards and follow manufacturer's instructions to iron them onto the card stock.

- Glue buttons or trim onto cards as desired.

- Use fine-point permanent-ink felt-tip pens to add details, stitching lines or words to the cards (see sketch).

Homespun Note Cards Procedure Page

HOMESPUN NOTE CARDS

Procedure

- Cut each piece of card stock in half to make two 5¹/₂ x8¹/₂-inch strips. Fold each strip in half to make a card.

- Follow manufacturer's instructions to apply fusible web to the back of fabric. **Note:** Fusible web may also be applied to pieces cut from scraps of fabric, which make nice backgrounds or borders for print figures or objects.

- Cut out fabric figures or objects. Arrange on cards and follow manufacturer's instructions to iron them onto the card stock.

- Glue buttons or trim onto cards as desired.

- Use fine-point permanent-ink felt-tip pens to add details, stitching lines or words to the cards (see sketch).

NOTE BOARD

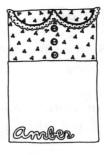

In our hectic lives, it can be difficult to keep track of all the little papers and self-adhesive notes we accumulate in our quest to stay organized! This Note Board is an attractive and practical way to keep those papers and notes all in one place.

Materials

For each person, you will need

- ❑ Photocopy of Note Board Procedure Page

- ❑ 10x12-inch piece of print fabric

- ❑ 10x15-inch piece of foam board

- ❑ 10x12-inch piece of coordinating denim or solid-colored fabric

- ❑ 6-inch piece of ribbon

- ❑ Three buttons

- ❑ 18-inch length of lace, rickrack or other trim. **Note:** Provide a variety of trims so that women can personalize according to their personal taste.

Additional Supplies

- ❑ Measuring sticks

- ❑ Scissors for cutting fabric

- ❑ Mat knife

- ❑ Hot-glue gun and hot-glue sticks

- ❑ Scraps of fabric, lace and trim

- ❑ **Optional:** fabric paint, in bottles with applicator tips

Preparation

- Photocopy Note Board Procedure Page for each person.

- Cut print fabric, foam board, denim or solid-colored fabric and ribbon to specified sizes.

Procedure

- Place print fabric right-side down. Lay foam board over it (see sketch a). Glue the corners and edges of print fabric to the back of the board.

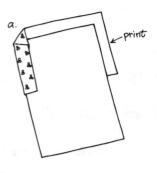

- Turn down 1/2 inch of one 12-inch edge of solid-colored or denim fabric and glue to hold (see sketch b).

- Place denim or solid-colored fabric right-side down, with the folded edge farthest from you. Lay foam board over fabric as shown in sketch b. Glue the corners and edges of fabric to the back of the board.

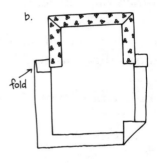

- Glue buttons and fabric, lace and trim scraps on the front of the board.

- Glue both ends of a 6-inch piece of ribbon to the top of the back side of the note board to make a hanger.

- **Optional:** Use fabric paint to add a message, name or design to the board.

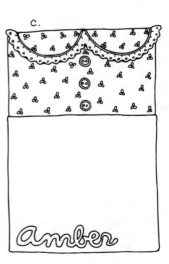

Note: The edge where the solid fabric overlaps the print fabric can be used as a pocket to hold a pen, or it can be glued closed. Use tacks or short push pins to attach notes to the board.

NOTE BOARD

Procedure

- Place print fabric right-side down. Lay foam board over it (see sketch a). Glue the corners and edges of print fabric to the back of the board.

- Turn down 1/2 inch of one 12-inch edge of solid-colored or denim fabric and glue to hold (see sketch b).

- Place denim or solid-colored fabric right-side down, with the folded edge farthest from you. Lay foam board over fabric as shown in sketch b. Glue the corners and edges of fabric to the back of the board.

- Glue buttons and fabric, lace and trim scraps on the front of the board.

- Glue both ends of a 6-inch piece of ribbon to the top of the back side of the note board to make a hanger.

- **Optional:** Use fabric paint to add a message, name or design to the board.

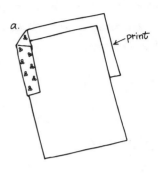

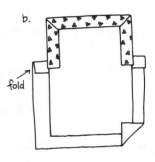

> **Note:** The edge where the solid fabric over-laps the print fabric can be used as a pocket to hold a pen, or it can be glued closed. Use tacks or short push pins to attach notes to the board.

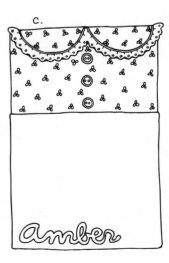

PASTA GIFT

The Pasta Gift makes a beautiful decoration, or it can be given as an edible gift. You may desire to attach your favorite lasagna recipe to the underside of the package.

Materials

For each person, you will need

- ❑ Photocopy of Pasta Gift Procedure Page
- ❑ 15-inch square of clear cellophane
- ❑ Five 2-foot-long pieces of raffia
- ❑ 6-inch length of 22-gauge floral wire
- ❑ 6 sun-dried tomatoes
- ❑ 6 bay leaves
- ❑ 9 lasagna noodles
- ❑ 2 small dried chilies
- ❑ 1 large dried chili
- ❑ 1 dry pearl onion (not canned)
- ❑ Sprig of fresh rosemary or oregano
- ❑ **Optional:** a blank recipe card

Additional Supplies

- ❑ Measuring stick
- ❑ Scissors for cutting paper
- ❑ Wire cutters
- ❑ Transparent tape
- ❑ **Optional:** Pens

Preparation

- Photocopy Pasta Gift Procedure Page for each person.

- Cut cellophane, raffia and floral wire to specified sizes.

Procedure

- In the center of the clear cellophane, arrange sun-dried tomatoes and bay leaves in an area the size of a lasagna noodle (see sketch a).

- Stack lasagna noodles over the tomatoes and bay leaves.

- Wrap cellophane around the noodles like a gift; secure with transparent tape.

- Use raffia to tie a bow around the width of the noodles (see sketch b).

- Use floral wire to wrap together the stem ends of the three chilies. Leave a 2-inch length of wire extending from the chilies.

- Slide the 2-inch end of wire up under the raffia bow and poke the end of the wire into the pearl onion. This will hold the chilies and onion on the gift.

- Slide the sprig of rosemary or oregano behind the onion and chilies (see sketch b).

- **Optional:** Write your favorite lasagna recipe on a recipe card and slide it under the raffia on the underside of the gift. Use tape to hold card in place.

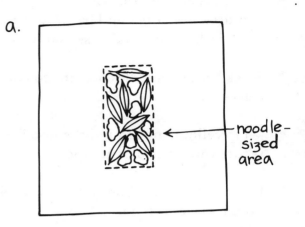

a.

noodle-sized area

b. onion

PASTA GIFT

Procedure

- In the center of the clear cellophane, arrange sun-dried tomatoes and bay leaves in an area the size of a lasagna noodle (see sketch a).

- Stack lasagna noodles over the tomatoes and bay leaves.

- Wrap cellophane around the noodles like a gift; secure with transparent tape.

- Use raffia to tie a bow around the width of the noodles (see sketch b).

- Use floral wire to wrap together the stem ends of the three chilies. Leave a 2-inch length of wire extending from the chilies.

- Slide the 2-inch end of wire up under the raffia bow and poke the end of the wire into the pearl onion. This will hold the chilies and onion on the gift.

- Slide the sprig of rosemary or oregano behind the onion and chilies (see sketch b).

- **Optional:** Write your favorite lasagna recipe on a recipe card and slide it under the raffia on the underside of the gift. Use tape to hold card in place.

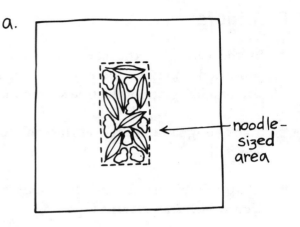

a.

noodle-sized area

b. onion

WESTERN SOUP MIX

This delicious soup is great any time of the year! You may wish to prepare a batch of Western Soup before the women arrive so that they can taste the finished product as they prepare the bags. Once again, this mix is a great gift or bazaar item.

Materials

For each person, you will need

- ❑ Photocopy of Western Soup Mix Procedure Page

For the Bag

- ❑ Western Soup Mix Recipe Master
- ❑ Colored card stock
- ❑ 18-inch length of lightweight jute
- ❑ Bandana or 18-inch piece of western-print fabric
- ❑ **Optional:** Wooden spoon

For the Mix

- ❑ 1 c. pearl barley
- ❑ 1 c. dried lentils
- ❑ 1 bay leaf
- ❑ 2 tbsp. dried minced onions
- ❑ 2 tbsp. parsley flakes
- ❑ 1 tbsp. basil
- ❑ 1 tbsp. thyme
- ❑ 1 tbsp. oregano
- ❑ $1\frac{1}{2}$ tsp. garlic powder
- ❑ $\frac{1}{2}$ tsp. ginger
- ❑ Quart-sized resealable plastic bag

Additional Supplies

- ❑ Measuring stick
- ❑ Scissors for cutting fabric
- ❑ Pinking shears
- ❑ Clean plastic bins
- ❑ Measuring cups and spoons
- ❑ Self-adhesive labels and a pen
- ❑ Disposable food-service gloves
- ❑ Scissors for cutting paper
- ❑ Hole punch

Preparation

- Photocopy Soup Mix Procedure Page for each person.

- Photocopy the Western Soup Mix Recipe Master onto colored card stock.

- Cut lightweight jute to specified size.

- Use pinking shears to cut western-print fabric to specified size.

- Place each mix ingredient in a clean bin and provide the appropriate measuring utensil. **Note:** Ingredients do not need to be dumped into the bins; just place the product package in the bin so that the bin can catch spills.

- Label each bin with the quantity of the ingredient each mix requires.

- Place food-service gloves and resealable bags beside the bins.

Procedure

- Wearing disposable food-service gloves, scoop appropriate quantities of mix ingredients into the resealable bag. Close bag securely.

- Place the bag in the center of the bandana or wrong side of fabric square. Gather the bandana around the bag and tie with the jute. **Optional:** Tie the handle of a wooden spoon along with the bandana.

- Cut out the recipe card and punch hole as indicated.

- Thread one end of jute through hole in recipe card and then tie ends of jute into a bow to secure card.

WESTERN SOUP MIX

Procedure

- Wearing disposable food-service gloves, scoop appropriate quantities of mix ingredients into the resealable bag. Close bag securely.

- Place the bag in the center of the bandana or wrong side of fabric square. Gather the bandana around the bag and tie with the jute. **Optional:** Tie the handle of a wooden spoon along with the bandana.

- Cut out the recipe card and punch hole as indicated.

- Thread one end of jute through hole in recipe card and then tie ends of jute into a bow to secure card.

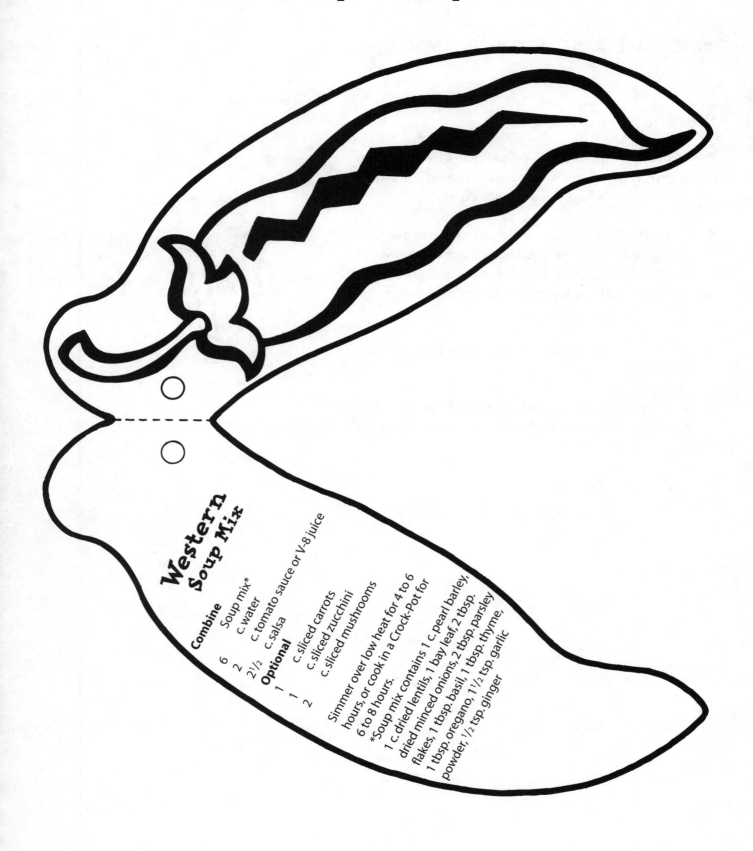

Western Soup Mix

Combine

Soup mix*
6   c. water
2   c. tomato sauce or V-8 juice
2½   c. salsa

Optional

1   c. sliced carrots
1   c. sliced zucchini
2   c. sliced mushrooms

Simmer over low heat for 4 to 6 hours, or cook in a Crock-Pot for 6 to 8 hours.

*Soup mix contains 1 c. pearl barley, 1 c. dried lentils, 1 bay leaf, 2 tbsp. dried minced onions, 2 tbsp. parsley flakes, 1 tbsp. basil, 1 tbsp. thyme, 1 tbsp. oregano, 1½ tsp. thyme, powder, ½ tsp. ginger

GIVING-BACK SERVICE PROJECTS

Working together to meet the needs of others is one of the most rewarding experiences you can provide for women. They will grow in love for each other and for Christ as they selflessly give to others. The community, your church body and the Kingdom will benefit from their gifts of service. Women can form strong bonds of fellowship while working together on a project, even while preparing the materials.

The first step in planning service projects is to prayerfully identify the needs and opportunities in your community and on the mission field. Choose projects that will minister in a way that is not already being done by other people. Because women are relational, reach out to others on a personal level, not just in material ways. Reaching out to others will create an opportunity for spiritual growth.

The next step in planning service projects is to assess the abilities, gifts and interests of the women you want to involve. Most women enjoy serving in ways that are an extension of who they are and what they have to offer. No woman wants to be forced into a situation that is not appropriate for her. However, it is important to provide opportunities that will take women out of their comfort zones and help them to learn to rely on the Lord.

The last step is to plan carefully. Doing a project with excellence is satisfying and successful and honors the one you ultimately serve: Christ. Know your financial limitations and keep a careful account of your resources. Set up leadership that can organize and inspire the women involved in the projects. Cover every project with prayer and incorporate opportunities for reflection and spiritual discussion as you prepare for and share the work.

chapter twelve

LOVING THE HOMELESS

If you are sharing these items with a rescue mission or other established organization, check with the organization's leadership to see what items they feel are appropriate. If you will be giving these out on the street, notify local law enforcement and social service agencies.

PERSONAL CARE KITS

Collect new personal care items that can be assembled into kits to share with needy individuals. Items you may want to include are

- ❑ Adhesive bandages

- ❑ Comb or brush

- ❑ Dental floss

- ❑ Deodorant

- ❑ Hand lotion

- ❑ Nail file

- ❑ Perfume/cologne samples

- ❑ Razor

- ❑ Shampoo and conditioner

- ❑ Soap

- ❑ Toothbrush and toothpaste

- ❑ Socks

- ❑ Washcloth

Purchase small plastic boxes or bags with zippers or sew drawstring bags to use as containers for your kits. **Optional:** Sturdy gallon-sized plastic bags with zip-type closures could also be used—an economic option if you are preparing a lot of kits. Where appropriate, include a small Bible, book or other word of encouragement.

BLANKETS OF LOVE

Collect warm, lightweight blankets (rather than comforters) that are in good condition. Carefully fold and roll each blanket into a warm bundle and tie with rope, $1/2$ inch elastic or colorful cord. Place each blanket in a plastic bag (such as a kitchen trash bag) and tie closed with a ribbon and a gift tag. Sleeping bags can also be collected.

Optional: Sew a pocket onto each blanket and insert a small Bible, book or word of love. Or create washable labels that carry a message of love and sew them onto each blanket.

HEAD-TO-TOE WARMTH

Collect jackets, knit hats, mittens or gloves, and new socks. Tuck a hat, a pair of mittens or gloves and a pair of socks into the pocket of each jacket. Include a Bible, book or word of encouragement as appropriate. Fold and wrap each jacket or place it in a gift bag and tie with a ribbon.

THE GIFT OF TIME

Volunteering on a regular basis in a homeless shelter, rescue mission or shelter for abused women is an effective personal way to express God's love for those in need. The women in your group can work together to provide much-needed service in a variety of ways, such as cleaning, cooking, serving or just being a listening ear to those in need of one.

chapter thirteen

CARING FOR MOMS IN CRISIS

QUILTS OF LOVE

Use the talents of your creative sewers to make handmade baby quilts for a local crisis pregnancy center or maternity home. Embroider a verse or blessing on a square to express love to the mother and child who will benefit from your group's efforts. Women can be involved in this project in different ways: donating materials, hosting quilting bees at their homes, cutting materials for the quilts, sewing or wrapping completed quilts. Pray for those who will be receiving each quilt.

SHOWERS OF BLESSING

Collect new baby items (e.g., clothes, blankets, diapers, wipes, bottles, toys). A gift certificate specifically for the mom also adds a nice touch. Place all the items in a colorful plastic laundry basket. Include a personal note, Bible, new mother's devotional or other appropriate materials—contact a crisis pregnancy center for suggestions. Tie a big ribbon on the basket and share it with a needy mom.

Your local crisis pregnancy center or maternity home can help you identify women in need. If possible, involve the women of your group in delivering the gifts.

ADOPT-A-MOM

Identify a mom—a single mom would be especially appreciative—in your congregation or community who would benefit from the personal support of the women in your group. Get to know the mom and identify meaningful ways you can meet needs in her life. Provide her with a meal, free child care, a carpet-cleaning service, a gift certificate to a hair salon, an oil change for her car or a scholarship to a retreat or seminar at which child care is provided. Surround the mom with prayer, encouragement and practical support.

Some new mothers may not have a female relative close by to lend support during times when she is overwhelmed with countless responsibilities and worries. Recruit women in your group to be there for her during those times or when she needs an afternoon off.

CRISIS PREGNANCY CENTERS

Contact a local crisis pregnancy center and find out its needs. Look beyond financial needs for ways the women in your group can be personally involved. For example, your group could adopt a room at the center to fix up and decorate, form a prayer group to personally pray for the staff by name or provide cleaning or office services. Group members can help raise funds for the center or provide child care for Bible studies.

If your community doesn't have a crisis pregnancy center, contact a local hospital or social service agency and offer help.

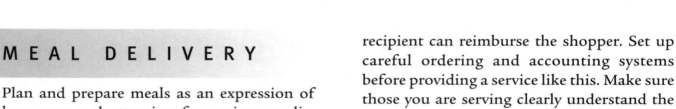

chapter fourteen

HONORING SENIORS AND THE DISABLED

MEAL DELIVERY

Plan and prepare meals as an expression of love, care and attention for seniors or disabled persons in your congregation or community. The women in your group can take turns preparing meals on a regular or temporary basis, depending on the need of the person they are serving and the resources of your group. When delivering a meal, encourage the group members to take time to visit and pray for those to whom they are reaching out.

ERRAND ANGELS

Many people can function in their own homes, but because of health or transportation limitations, they find shopping difficult. This service can be done on a one-on-one basis, or it can be done on a larger scale. If resources permit, obtain itemized lists from those you are serving and make purchases for them. Upon delivery of purchased items, the recipient can reimburse the shopper. Set up careful ordering and accounting systems before providing a service like this. Make sure those you are serving clearly understand the financial responsibilities of participating in the program.

RIDE ALONG

Make a list of women who are willing to provide a ride to someone with a transportation need. Rides can be provided for doctor appointments, visits to the bank, shopping, etc. Designate a coordinator to develop the list of drivers and to make sure that all drivers are safe drivers and are properly insured. Contact people who you feel can benefit from these services and offer to provide these services to them. Have them contact the coordinator, who will then notify a driver who will meet that need. Do not publish the names and numbers of the drivers for their protection and to avoid abuse of their service.

HELPING HANDS

Many people with physical limitations spend a significant amount of time without personal contact. Provide opportunities in which the women of your group visit with these people. The women of your group can simply spend time talking with them, reading to them, helping them with correspondence or paperwork, watching a movie with them or having a cup of coffee and sharing a time of prayer.

TOASTY TOES

Get quilters, crocheters or knitters together to make lap quilts or afghans for those with physical limitations. Women can work individually or have a quilting, crocheting and/or knitting party! As much as possible, personalize each quilt by incorporating favorite colors or embroidering the recipient's name on a square. Allow the women to share in the joy of presenting their gifts to the recipients. These quilts or afghans can also be distributed at a retirement or convalescent home, but first contact the facility to make sure the items are needed.

TRAY FAVORS

Making tray favors for use at a local convalescent hospital or retirement center can really brighten the residents' days. Scented items such as potpourri wrapped in festive fabric and tied with ribbon work well, as do small silk flowers or ribbons attached to a napkin ring and accompanied by a personal note. Keep the items small and simple yet bright and cheerful. Contact the convalescent hospital or retirement center staff to make arrangements. Be sure to inquire with the caretakers before providing candy or food items.

chapter fifteen

COMING ALONGSIDE— RESPONDING TO LIFE EVENTS

COOKING CO-OP

The Cooking Co-op is an opportunity for women to spend an evening enjoying each other's company while providing a meal for a family that has experienced a loss, has a member recovering from an illness or surgery or has just brought home a newborn. Host the evening of cooking in a home or use your church's kitchen. Organize the event so that each woman involved provides a portion of the ingredients for making the meal. You may want to cook enough food so that the women who are preparing the meal can also taste their efforts. Purchase disposable containers for delivering the food so that the family doesn't have to return any dishes. **Note:** Inform the family ahead of time that you will be providing a meal. Be sensitive to any diet restrictions or food allergies the family may have.

COLLEGE SURVIVAL KITS

Heading off to college—even if in the same town—is a time of transition for young people. Show love and support for these often overlooked members of your congregation. Assemble items that will encourage them and make them feel connected to home. Include a Bible or Christian book, gift certificates and coupons to popular restaurants, a phone card, treats and toiletries. Research groups and churches in the college area that have healthy ministries aimed at college students and provide that information to the student. Arrange the items in a plastic tote or laundry bag, tie a big bow around it and include a personal note of care and prayer support.

Obtain addresses (including e-mail addresses) of these students and send them notes of encouragement throughout the school year.

Each woman in the group could adopt a student to encourage during the year.

SECRET PEN PAL

Many teenaged girls in your church's youth group may not have a strong spiritual influence in their home or they may be going through a rough time in their relationship with their parents. Ask your church's youth leader to provide names and addresses of teenaged girls who could benefit from the loving influence of a godly woman and who would be interested in having a secret pen pal to encourage and pray for her and answer her questions. Provide a mailbox in the youth meeting room for the girls to deposit their letters and then give the letters to the women in your group who have said they want to participate. Each woman could be assigned a specific girl to encourage through the year, or different women could respond to the girls' letters. The women could also send cards to the girls for birthdays and holidays throughout the year. Spending regular time in prayer for these girls should be an ongoing ministry of your women's group.

GIFT BAGS

Assemble gift bags that are appropriate for various life events. Ask local businesses and members of your congregation to donate the contents and/or coupons. Make these bags available to the women in your church to share with others. Women can take these bags, personalize them and personally share them with others. Choose a theme and color for each bag to simplify distribution. Theme ideas and gift contents might include the following:

- **Your New Baby**—bib, socks, bottle, diaper or baby-care coupons, appropriate book or devotional material, a list of groups that help new moms stay connected or find support, etc.

- **Welcome Neighbor**—invitation to dinner at your house, coupons for local restaurants or stores, a calendar, etc. Personalize by adding a small potted plant or a bag of homemade cookies.

- **Wedding Wishes**—appropriate Christian book on marriage or small photo album, recipe cards for sharing favorite recipes, CD of romantic music, two movie passes, etc. Personalize the gift by writing recipes on the recipe cards.

- **You Made It! (Graduation)**—CD of Christian music, gas card, phone card, fast-food coupons or gift certificates, a key chain, a devotional, etc.

- **Empty Nest**—devotional book, writing paper and pen, restaurant gift certificate, two movie passes, etc.

- **Thinking of You**—small arrangement of silk flowers, potpourri, candle, candy, phone card, CD of uplifting music, etc.

- **Good for You!**—party poppers, balloons, candy, food coupons or gift certificates, movie passes, etc. to celebrate a milestone or holiday.

INTERNET CONNECTION

Involve your technically inclined women by setting up an Internet bulletin board for your women's ministry. Women may share inspiring stories or prayer requests. Assign a number to each subscribing woman so that prayer requests can be shared anonymously if desired. Women can submit information via e-mail to a designated webmaster. Before posting any requests or information, the webmaster should check them for appropriateness. This is a great way to keep shut-ins, missionaries and out-of-towners connected.

EVENTS TO REMEMBER

Providing women with memorable opportunities to enjoy each other and build relationships will create an environment of growth and support.

This section describes informal small-group events, structured large-group gatherings and ways to make retreats unforgettable. These suggestions will help you set the stage for introducing your women to a deeper walk with God and closer fellowship with one another.

Whenever women are gathered, it is helpful to have leaders involved who can stimulate conversation while being sensitive to women who communicate a need for a friend or a listening ear. Some of the events include discussion starters that will help small-group leaders or hostesses facilitate interaction among the women participating.

When appropriate, ask women who attend the events to complete and return the Friendship Card (see page 150). This tool will help you know more about the women you are serving and will allow them to communicate their needs to you. Small-group leaders (or the women running the check-in table) can distribute the cards and collect them at the end of an event.

chapter sixteen

SMALL-GROUP EVENTS

These events are designed for groups ranging from 4 to 12 people. An informal, small-group setting is a unique opportunity for the women to get to know each other more personally. If you have a large women's ministry, these events could be targeted at a specific segment of your ministry: single moms, Bible study leadership, military spouses, etc. Or you could put together a group of women based on interests or their Bible study small group.

COOKING TOGETHER

Women love to learn from each other in the kitchen. Choose a menu that will give the women an opportunity to try something new. Make sure you have a "chef in charge" who is familiar with the foods and recipes that the women will be preparing. The women can either supply the necessary ingredients for the evening, or they can contribute their portion of the cost and one person can do the shopping. Determine the quantity of food needed by calculating the total number of servings desired, based on whether the prepared meal will be shared by the group or whether each woman will be taking home a particular number of servings to share with her family. If women will be taking the food home, instruct them to bring appropriate dishes or containers. Before the event, photocopy the recipes so that they are available for the women to take home.

Options

- The meal could be prepared as a ministry to others: providing a meal for someone who is ill, who has lost a loved one or who has had a baby. Before planning the meal, however, ask the person to be served if he or she would welcome a meal and if he or she has any dietary restrictions.

- Rather than cooking a whole meal, the group could bake bread, make cookies or other special treats. These options might be especially appropriate at holiday times. The women could make the treats and freeze them for future use or give them as gifts. Be sure to provide resealable freezer bags or other containers in which to take the baked items home.

MUSIC TO YOUR EARS

Singing together in praise, worship or simply for entertainment draws women together in a unique way. It also provides an outlet for those who love music. Go Christmas caroling together at a retirement home or convalescent hospital or sing around your church's neighborhood. Provide a gift bag of cookies with your Christmas cheer at each home. This event doesn't have to be limited to Christmas time! Gather around a piano at a rescue mission, a women's prison or a children's home and have a hymn sing or praise time, or simply have a crazy night of karaoke, snacks and laughter at your church.

SLEEPOVERS

Be kids again with an old-fashioned slumber party! This is a great bonding time for a small group of women from a Bible study, leadership team, moms of teenagers in your youth group—you name it! Arrange the sleepover in someone's home at a time when children and men will not be present so that the women can relax, get a little crazy and get to know each other. Plan a few flexible activities or crowd breakers (see pp. 154-171 for ideas) to get things going. When bedtime comes (if ever), women like to be comfortable. Have adequate sleeping accommodations away from the party scene for your early birds. A delicious breakfast is a nice ending to your fun together. Another option is have the sleepover in a hotel suite or mountain retreat. Some of your more adventurous women might even like to go camping together.

GAME NIGHT

Providing structure in a fun setting allows all temperaments of women to mix and get acquainted. Games like Bunko, Charades,

Pictionary or Outburst provide opportunities for fun and interaction. Allow those who want to stay out of the game action to be involved by arranging snacks, working a puzzle, just chatting or watching the action.

MOVIE NIGHT

There are many movies that are enjoyed most in a women-only setting. Spouses will probably be glad to miss out on enduring another girl movie or "chick flick." Make use of a home or facility with a big-screen or projection TV. Have women bring floor pillows, bean-bag chairs, etc. Provide tissues, popcorn, soft drinks and tea and coffee.

EXERCISE GROUPS

For women, sticking to a resolution to exercise is more successful when we have accountability and encouragement. Provide the women with names and contact information of those interested in leading a particular group: walking, jogging, cycling, swimming, aerobics, spinning, kickboxing, etc. Set up times and places where they can meet and exercise together. You may also want to arrange accountability partners who can call and encourage each other to persevere.

RECIPE EXCHANGE

New ideas for the menu are always welcome. This event can be organized on a small or large scale. Depending on the number of women involved, gather in a home or at church. Have each participant prepare a favorite food item and multiple copies of the recipe. Enjoy tasting the different dishes and talking over cooking techniques and ingredients. The women can collect the recipes that they are interested in trying at home.

Options

- Plan ahead and compile the recipes into a booklet to distribute.

- Have a theme for the recipes to be shared (e.g., Christmas cookies, Easter breads, breakfasts/brunches, ethnic meals)

HOT TUB AND NACHO PARTY

If you have access to a hot tub, gather a small group of women to enjoy its warmth and each other's company. Warm robes to snuggle up in after soaking and maybe even a roaring fire in a fire pit add the perfect touch. Put together a build-your-own-nachos bar for snack time, having the women provide the various ingredients.

SECRET ANGELS

Help your small groups connect on a more personal level by setting up secret angels. Each woman draws a name of another woman in the group and keeps the name she has drawn a secret. Each woman anonymously gives small gifts or thoughtful notes of encouragement to the woman whose name she drew. Decide on a set amount of time for the giving—a year or at least the school year probably works best, but you could do it for only one month or during a special time such as Lent or an eight-week Bible study. Plan a time for the givers to reveal themselves to the receivers such as an end-of-the-year party or a special luncheon. You might want to allow the women to guess who their secret angel has been and to share appreciation for her angel's efforts.

chapter seventeen

LARGE-GROUP EVENTS

Large-group events come in a variety of shapes and sizes. Some are used as outreach opportunities to welcome unchurched women into fellowship. Some provide profound opportunities for praise, worship and spiritual growth for believers. The keys to a successful event are to know the purpose for the event and to have a clear understanding of whom you want to reach. All aspects of the event should then be designed to support this purpose and to reach the target group.

The large-group events described in this chapter can be tailored to fit the needs of your ministry. These ideas are appropriate for use at your church or other local setting although they could also be incorporated into a retreat. Each idea presents a theme, suggests Bible verses to support that theme and gives creative suggestions for food, decorations and stimulating conversation in small groups about the theme.

Fall Events

Harvest Tea

> *Open your eyes and look at the fields! They are ripe for harvest.*
> John 4:35

Theme: Touching Hearts for Jesus at Home and Abroad

This is a great opportunity to hear a missionary woman's story and for the women in your group to support her in prayer. Spotlight the different families and countries your church supports and share the personal stories and requests of each person or family. If possible, show items or dress in traditional clothing from these countries. Include local missionary efforts as well. Have printed information about different mission opportunities, but focus your event on the personal needs and insights of those you are supporting.

Decorating Ideas

Decorate with a harvest theme of fruits, vegetables and grains. Include several copies of the missionaries' stories at each table. Some missionaries have picture postcards or pamphlets that give basic information about them, their families and the mission.

Food Suggestions

Provide light snacks from a variety of countries (e.g., sushi, egg rolls, pastries, scones and clotted cream, tropical fruits). Ask the missionaries for suggestions.

Discussion Starters for Small Groups

- Have you visited other countries? Which ones and for what purpose?

- What adjustments would you need to make to live in the country you visited?

- What are some ways you think we could support a missionary in that country? Share a prayer list if you support a missionary from that country.

- What are the benefits of sharing Christ with others?

Precious in God's Sight Brunch

Come to me, all you who are weary and burdened, and I will give you rest.
Take my yoke upon you and learn from me, for I am gentle and humble in heart,
and you will find rest for your souls. For my yoke is easy and my burden is light.

Matthew 11:28-30

Theme: Helping Women Feel Special and Pampered

Moms have spent a summer of caring for children, working women are entitled to a Labor Day break, and seniors can be valued for their selfless giving and wisdom. Provide fresh flowers, small appreciation gifts or pampering experiences for women to enjoy—such as a manicure, a makeover, a chair massage, or a hair-and-skin-care demonstration. A short message on Psalm 139; Matthew 11:28-30 or 1 John 3:1 will help women focus on the precious care God provides for His beloved. Appropriate background music will set a tone of rest and peace.

Decorating Ideas

Create a "tools of the trade" display on each table. Assign a profession to each table and create a centerpiece comprising the tools used to perform that job. Table themes may include stay-at-home mom, retirement, education, business, service providers (medical, retail, restaurant, etc.), creative arts, etc.

Provide broad categories so that you will have more than one person at each table but not so broad that everyone is sitting at the same table! Customize the categories to the women you serve.

Food Suggestions

Brunch dishes that are both hot and cold will help women feel pampered. Variety and abundance will communicate this as well. Having the brunch catered may further pamper the women. If that is not possible, look in to having the men or youth do the cooking and/or serving.

Discussion Starters for Small Groups

- What expressions of love and appreciation are meaningful to you?

- Share a time when someone made you feel special.

- Whom would you like to show appreciation to in a special way?

Thanksgiving Breakfast or Luncheon

Theme: Thankfulness/ Recipe Exchange

Have the women bring their favorite seasonal recipes and collect them as the women arrive. As the women share lunch, reproduce the recipes into booklets that the women can take home. Have different readers share poems, stories or Scripture that illustrate thankfulness. Spend time singing praise songs and sharing prayers of thanksgiving.

Decorating Ideas

Cover the tables with fall print tablecloths or runners. For centerpieces, remove the tops of small pumpkins, clean out the insides of the pumpkins and use them as bases for fresh or dried flower arrangements. Raffle the centerpieces or offer them for sale after your event.

Food Suggestions

Keep the meal light. Include fall foods such as apple crisp, muffins, pumpkin bread, bagels and cream cheese, cheese cubes and deviled eggs for breakfast. Or provide a salad bar with an assortment of breads or sandwich makings and a light dessert. Keep beverages simple: coffee, tea, water and juice.

Discussion Starters for Small Groups

- How would you like to celebrate Thanksgiving this year?

- What family traditions do you enjoy at Thanksgiving?

- What new traditions would you like to start?

- What has been your greatest blessing this year?

Christmas Dinner

> *"The virgin will be with child and will give birth to a son, and they will call him Immanuel"—which means, "God with us."*
>
> Matthew 1:23

Theme: God with Us

Share a favorite Christmas story that illustrates God's love and care for His people. You could have a woman play Mary, the mother of Jesus, telling her story about trusting God using Matthew 1:18-23 and Luke 2:1-40. Music can have a great impact during this season, so make a special effort to provide a quality, meaningful presentation.

Decorating Ideas

Give your best effort to create a warm, seasonal environment. You may want to bring the outdoors in using trees, fences, lampposts and animal figures. Cover tables with green or white tablecloths; use small evergreens for centerpieces; and add a touch of red with poinsettias, bows or apples. Keep the houselights low enough to allow holiday candles and Christmas lights to illuminate the room.

Food Suggestions

This is a great opportunity to provide a fancy, catered meal. If your budget is limited, you might opt for a buffet, delegating the cooking to several volunteers. Sell tickets to cover food costs and to get an accurate head count of those women planning to attend the dinner.

Discussion Starters for Small Groups

- Share a favorite Christmas memory.

- What can you do to focus your Christmas on God's love through His gift of Jesus?

- Tell about a time when you saw God's care for you or a loved one.

New Year Soup Supper

Theme: New Beginnings

Ask several women to share their stories of how God has given them a new start in life. You might ask a pastor's wife or an older woman whose story is not familiar to most of the group to share her story. Invite a woman from your group to share a song that illustrates a meaningful time of growing in faith.

Decorating Ideas

Use flags, banners, whistles, trophies, ribbons and other symbols of an important sporting competition such as the Olympics to set the tone.

Food Suggestions

Organize a soup supper that includes a variety of soups, stews, breads and salads. The women can either purchase tickets, or they can purchase admission by bringing a pot of homemade soup or a salad to share. Make sure the women indicate whether they will be bringing food when they register for the event.

Discussion Starters for Small Groups

- What life events can provide an opportunity to make a new start?

- What challenges are involved in starting something new?

- How has God provided you with an opportunity to make a new start?

Valentine Mother/Daughter Pie Social

> *This is how God showed his love among us: He sent his one and only Son into the world that we might live through him. We love because he first loved us.*
>
> 1 John 4:9,19

Theme: God's Great Love

Focus on the limitless love of God as expressed through His gift to us: Jesus Christ. Because this is a mother/daughter event, you may have women from many walks of life attending. Be sensitive to this mixed crowd and treat this as an outreach event, not as an evangelism opportunity. Younger participants may enjoy a craft project such as wrapping an inexpensive stick ballpoint pen and the stem of a silk flower with floral tape to make a flower pen. Provide note cards and envelopes for women to express love and appreciation to others. Teach the women and girls how to sing "Jesus Loves Me" in sign language. For inspiration, have several women share their love stories. Because not all the women will be married, try to incorporate stories of single women who have experienced God's sustaining love through the years. The love stories can be shared as a slide show, a video presentation or as live interviews.

Decorating Ideas

Flowers and lace are the perfect backdrop for a pie social. Use doilies or lace tablecloths over solid-colored tablecloths to brighten the room. Incorporate an individual flower for each woman in your table decorations. For example, you could fill a clear vase with many single-stemmed flowers, or you could place a single flower in a votive jar at each woman's place setting. A mirror under each centerpiece adds a sparkling touch. Set up the pie table by laying a cloth over boxes of different heights and shapes. Set the pies on these surfaces for display and arrange fresh flowers in between.

Food Suggestions

Provide a large variety of pies, either homemade or purchased from a bakery. Cut the pies in small slices, so the mothers and daughters will feel free to sample more than one type. Have several women designated as servers to keep mess to a minimum and to assist younger participants. Include both hot and cold beverages, including milk for the younger children.

Discussion Starters for Small Groups

- What are the best ways a person can show you that he or she loves you?

- How do you like to express love to others?

- How does experiencing God's love help you love others?

Easter Breakfast

If anyone would come after me, he must deny himself and take up his cross and follow me. For whoever wants to save his life will lose it, but whoever loses his life for me will find it. I tell you the truth, whatever you did for one of the least of these brothers of mine, you did for me.

Matthew 16:24-25; 25:40

Theme: Galilean Breakfast

Spend a quiet morning eating a light breakfast; then spend the rest of the time in prayer and worship. Have volunteers read sections of John 21. Focus this time on obedience and submission to Christ's command to take care of His sheep and to follow Him. Make it clear to the women that this will be a deep, spiritual time, not an outreach event. Because this is a time of worship and praise, there will be limited small-group discussion or casual conversation.

Decorating Ideas

Create a fisherman theme by incorporating nets, starfish, shells, palm branches, etc. If possible, have the women sit on the floor on blankets, but provide chairs for those who might have difficulty sitting on the floor.

Food Suggestions

Keep the food light and simple. Fruit, flat bread or crackers, juice, water and hot drinks will suffice.

Memorial Day Dinner

> *Love the* LORD *your God with all your heart and with all your soul and with all your strength. These commandments that I give you today are to be upon your hearts. Impress them on your children. Talk about them when you sit at home and when you walk along the road, when you lie down and when you get up.*
>
> Deuteronomy 6:5-7

Theme: Sharing Legacies and Honoring Heroes

Take time to honor the spiritual impact others have had on the lives of the women in your group. Arrange to have several women tell about the legacy of faith they inherited from previous generations. If available, show photos of significant people as the women share. Then have a time of "open mike" for women who want to briefly share about spiritually significant people in their lives. Read Deuteronomy 6:5-7 and Psalm 78:4 aloud. Talk about the impact sharing your faith with the next generation can have.

Decorating Ideas

Arrange wreaths of flowers that incorporate a collection of old photos of family and friends. Borrow the photos, make quality copies and return the originals. Cover round tables with traditional gingham or floral print cloths.

Food Suggestions

Prepare a traditional family-style meal with chicken, rice and vegetables, or roast beef with mashed potatoes and green beans. Serve the meal family style at each table.

Discussion Starters for Small Groups

- Share a memory of someone from your childhood who had a profound impact on your life.

- What are some ways to communicate values and spiritual truths to others?

- What values would you like to share with the next generation?

Celebrate Life Luncheon

> *Worship the LORD with gladness; come before him with joyful songs. Know that the LORD is God. It is he who made us, and we are his; we are his people, the sheep of his pasture. I will sing to the LORD all my life; I will sing praise to my God as long as I live. May my meditation be pleasing to him, as I rejoice in the LORD.*
>
> Psalm 100:2-3; 104:33-34

Theme: Celebrate Life!

Life is a precious gift to be enjoyed and used for God's glory. Select special music to communicate this message. Read appropriate poems, stories and Scripture passages between songs.

Decorating Ideas

Plant flowers or bedding plants in trays to make miniature gardens for the centerpieces. If available, place tabletop fountains around the room.

Food Suggestions

Create the ultimate salad bar and allow women to serve themselves. Include green salad ingredients, potato salad, macaroni salad and rolls or muffins. Top off the lunch with fruit juice served with frozen slices of peaches or grapes.

Discussion Starters for Small Groups

- How do you treat a gift differently from an ordinary possession?

- How does seeing life as a gift affect your enjoyment of it?

- If you knew your days on Earth were to end soon, how would you spend your time?

Fourth of July Ice-Cream Social

> *It is for freedom that Christ has set us free. Stand firm, then,*
> *and do not let yourselves be burdened again by a yoke of slavery.*
> Galatians 5:1

Theme: Freedom in Christ

Use this patriotic holiday to celebrate what true freedom is—the freedom we have through Christ. Ask a mature Christian who has experienced limited freedom through a disability or other life circumstance to share his or her story, or invite a Christian veteran to share his or her insights on the preciousness of freedom. Share traditional patriotic music peppered with songs of gratitude to God for His gift of abundant life. Since this is an old-fashioned ice-cream social, you may want to present the music in the form of a quartet.

Optional: Open this event to families and the rest of the congregation. Add a carnival, games or a picnic and finish up with ice cream. Proclaim the message of Christ's freedom through music and banners.

Decorating Ideas

Balloons and bunting everywhere! Also use white as a base color to give that ice-cream shop look. Set up a counter where participants can order their ice-cream sundaes and cones or root-beer floats.

Food Suggestions

Provide vanilla, chocolate and strawberry ice cream (homemade if possible) and a variety of toppings. Set up blenders for making milk shakes, have root beer for floats and be sure to include the whipped cream, cherries and chopped nuts to top everything off!

Discussion Starters for Small Groups

- How would you define freedom?

- What freedoms do people often take for granted?

- What are the benefits of being a slave to God?

Cruise Buffet

> *Let us not become weary in doing good, for at the proper time we will reap a harvest if we do not give up. Therefore, as we have opportunity, let us do good to all people, especially to those who belong to the family of believers.*
>
> Galatians 6:9-10

Theme: Building Family Memories

Share the importance of making family time a priority. Focus on the positive impact that time together as a family has on every family member. Invite a speaker to discuss ideas for building positive family memories. Encourage the women to tell humorous stories about past family vacations, holidays or other family-building events. This is a great event to invite unchurched friends and family members to, so keep it meaningful but light.

Decorating Ideas

Reproduce a cruise ship dining room. You can either make this a dress-up affair with white tablecloths, blue napkins and clear glass; or create a casual tropical scene with tiki torches, coconuts and flower motifs.

Food Suggestions

Set out a buffet table with a variety of tropical fruits, appetizers, finger foods and juice drinks (complete with little umbrellas and fruit skewers).

Discussion Starters for Small Groups

- What was your favorite family time as a child?

- How do you preserve memories from your family's time together?

- How can you incorporate faith and biblical instruction into your time together?

Box Lunch Picnic

> *Tremble before him, all the earth! The world is firmly established; it cannot be moved.*
> *Let the heavens rejoice, let the earth be glad; let them say among the nations, "The LORD*
> *reigns!" Let the sea resound, and all that is in it; let the fields be jubilant, and everything*
> *in them! Then the trees of the forest will sing, they will sing for joy before the LORD, for he*
> *comes to judge the earth. Give thanks to the LORD, for he is good; his love endures forever.*
>
> 1 Chronicles 16:30-34

Theme: Celebrate God in His Creation

Hold this event in an outside setting: a local park, a beach, a beautiful garden or someone's yard. Share a few words about enjoying God's creation and sing a few songs of praise. You may want to give each participant devotional material to use for quiet moments during the summer. Play soft background music for women to enjoy as they eat.

Decorating Ideas

The outdoor setting should fill most of your decorating needs. You may want to add hanging baskets of flowers, small fountains, benches or small tables at which women can eat.

Food Suggestions

Have each woman bring one boxed lunch (enough to serve one). Encourage women to make it creative, dressing it up with ribbons and special treats. Number each lunch and either have women draw numbers for their lunch or hold an auction—make it clear what the money collected will be used for, such as a mission project or providing nursery supplies. Provide ice-cold bottled water and juices. Women can sit at benches or small tables as they eat, share each other's company and enjoy God's creation.

Discussion Starters for Small Groups

- Where is your favorite place to enjoy silence?

- What things get in the way of finding quiet time with the Lord?

- What are the benefits of spending quiet time with God?

FRIENDSHIP CARD

We are so glad you are here! Please help us get to know you. We would love to assist you in any way we can—just let us know by filling out the appropriate spaces.

Name _____ Date _____

Home Phone _____ Work Phone _____

Street Address _____

City _____ State _____ Zip _____

E-Mail Address _____

❑   First-time visitor, guest of _____
❑   Returning guest
❑   Change of address, phone number or e-mail address

I would like more information about
❑   The church
❑   Women's ministries
❑   I want to be involved with _____

❑   Please call me.
❑   Please pray for me. (Write your request on the back of this card.)

FRIENDSHIP CARD

We are so glad you are here! Please help us get to know you. We would love to assist you in any way we can—just let us know by filling out the appropriate spaces.

Name _____ Date _____

Home Phone _____ Work Phone _____

Street Address _____

City _____ State _____ Zip _____

E-Mail Address _____

❑   First-time visitor, guest of _____
❑   Returning guest
❑   Change of address, phone number or e-mail address

I would like more information about
❑   The church
❑   Women's ministries
❑   I want to be involved with _____

❑   Please call me.
❑   Please pray for me. (Write your request on the back of this card.)

chapter eighteen

RETREAT ACTIVITIES

Retreats are a great way to bring your group to a deeper level of connectedness with one another and to deepen each woman's walk with the Lord. There are many ways to make a retreat memorable and positive. The following ideas will help your creative ideas stir.

Activity Ideas

Personal Contact

Designate women to be prayer warriors for those attending the retreat. These women may or may not be able to attend the retreat themselves. From the list of those registered, assign each attendee to a prayer warrior. Ask the warriors to pray faithfully and specifically for the assigned woman each day prior to the retreat as well as during the event. Ask them to pray for any specific needs they may be aware of, for God to prepare their hearts to hear His Word, to eliminate any roadblocks that may hinder them from attending and for safety during the event. Have each warrior write a personal note of welcome, encouragement and commitment to pray for her assigned woman. These notes can be given to the women as they check in at the retreat. If the prayer warrior is attending the retreat, have her personally greet the woman she has been praying for at some point during the retreat.

Mail Call

Set up a system for women to write to one another during the retreat. Provide note cards and envelopes for this purpose. Have a drop box for notes to be collected each morning and have them delivered to the women at dinnertime using a camp mail-call system. All women can make use of this opportunity, but especially the prayer warriors and leadership team should send a note of encouragement to each woman. This is a great way to communicate words of thanks, encouragement and appreciation to each other.

Time to Laugh

We all love to laugh! Play games, perform skits, read anecdotes and recite poems that illustrate the lighter side of the retreat theme. This is a good way to begin a session, followed by music and more serious material. Plan ahead and rehearse beforehand so that the laughter will be because of the content, not the presentation!

Library

Prior to the retreat, collect inspirational books, Christian magazines, good fiction, Bible study materials, etc. You may be able to get a local Christian bookstore or church members to donate them, or you can purchase some from a distributor or discount website. At the retreat, create a library area or free bookshop where women can sit and read or take books for personal use.

Party Time

Designate certain rooms as party rooms. Choose rooms that are set apart enough that noise will not be intrusive to those not participating. These rooms provide a place for the night owls to have fun away from the early birds who want to sleep in peace. The women staying in each party room act as hostesses for specific recreational activities during the evenings, such as board games, movies, karaoke, line dancing, makeovers, manicures or chocolate tasting! These are great ways for women to build friendships while having fun.

Gifts and Surprises

Women love to receive gifts and thoughtful surprises. Throughout the retreat, find ways to select women to receive gifts that you have put together. Gifts can include donated items and services from people in your church or items that you have purchased that relate to the theme. Honor some women for special talents or life events—new grandmother, special anniversary, etc.—or select women by a certain birthdate, by numbering chairs, by coding materials you supplied at check-in, etc. Have a gift corner and hostess. When a woman is selected, she can visit the corner and choose one item from those available.

Worship

Provide times of corporate worship before or after each teaching time. Most women's groups have at least one or two women capable of leading or playing an instrument, but you could also use audiocassettes or CDs to provide the music. Or for a change of pace, encourage a variety of forms of worship besides (or along with) music; include opportunities for artistic expression such as painting, drawing, writing, modeling clay, etc. You could also have women share testimonies related to your theme. Another idea would be to have women write their thoughts in silent worship. To encourage personal worship time, prepare a small devotional booklet with a Scripture passage, a question or two and a short prayer to allow the women to spend time alone with the Lord.

Seminars

Offer optional seminars on specific topics. After presenting the options during a large-group session, allow women the opportunity to sign up for these seminars. Sign-ups will help you prepare materials, provide adequate seating and limit participation if needed. Women from your church who have specific expertise in an area can lead the seminars. Seminar choices may include exploring the role of prayer and worship, women's health, parenting teenagers, marriage, journaling. You could also offer some light seminars such as learning a new skill or doing a craft. These could be offered during free time when some women might want to stay inside. Choose topics based on the women's interests and the availability of seminar leaders.

Guided Walks

Retreats usually don't lack opportunities to sit, but scheduled times to get up and move around are often neglected. By organizing hikes, walks or local tours, the women can move and rejuvenate. They will be more prepared to listen to the next teaching session after an invigorating walk outdoors.

Craft Ideas

Free time set aside for crafting can be a wonderful relationship builder. At a retreat, a longer expanse of time can be given to more time-consuming crafts that you might not have time for during regular weekday meetings. Have the women sign up for the specific craft activity before the retreat so that you can be prepared. However, have a few extras for those who might decide to join the class at the retreat. Here are a few suggestions to get you thinking.

Watercolor Painting

Women enjoy being creative and learning something new. Provide materials and creative guidance as women express themselves through painting. You can create a watercolor painting station in a meeting room, or take the supplies outdoors to a nearby garden or picturesque setting. Wherever you choose to set up the painting studio, be sure to have adequate supplies, such as paints, watercolor paper, pencils, brushes, containers for water and paper towels. If taking your artists outside, for each woman provide a large piece of Masonite and clips to hold the paper to the board.

Jewelry Making

Creating simple pieces of jewelry is easy and fun. Women can assemble earrings, necklaces, pendants or bracelets to take home with them. Supplies are available from most craft stores. You will need clear thread for stringing necklaces, hardware (clasps, hooks, posts and clips) and wire posts for beaded pendants. You will also need to borrow a few needle-nose pliers and collect beads from broken necklaces or thrift stores or purchase them new.

Designing Scrapbooks

This activity would require women to come prepared with pictures and mementos, so plan ahead. Suggest a theme to avoid anyone bringing 25 years' worth of photos to arrange in two hours. Possible themes might be "The Year in Review, " "Christmas at Our House," "My Life" or do an individual page for each family member (include pets). Be sensitive to the life situations of the women, especially those who do not have families.

Stamping

This is a fun activity for everyone and has a variety of possible projects such as greeting cards, letterhead or decorative items. You might have some women in your group who have collections of stamps that they would be willing to lend to you for the retreat. Or you might enlist an instructor from a local craft store.

For more information about planning retreats, refer to *The Focus on the Family Women's Ministry Guide.*

chapter nineteen

COMMUNITY BUILDERS AND CROWD BREAKERS

A community builder is any activity that promotes the deeper sense of the group among its members. Visitors need an opportunity to become part of the group as soon as possible. Longtime members need to know that they continue to have an important part in the group. Community-building activities are great for accomplishing all of these goals.

Crowd breakers, also known as ice breakers, can be brief activities used at the beginning of a session to warm up the group, or they can be longer activities, taking the entire meeting time to complete. The purpose is to push the women in your group out of their comfort zones or cliques to become acquainted with others and increase the opportunity to build new relationships.

Materials Needed

None

Procedure

Explain to the women that they will walk around and mingle until you yell out a number. They are then to form a group with that number of people in it. For example if you yell "Six!" the women must stop and grab five other people to form small groups of six members each. When they do form the group of six, they are to sit down. If any group has more or less than six, they are out of the game and must sit on the sidelines. Then when you say "Mingle," the remaining women start mingling again until the leader calls out another number, say three. This is repeated until there are only two people left.

Variation

You could expand on this idea by using this as a means to form discussion groups. These discussion groups could be formed to discuss just one topic or to form a group for a Bible study discussion. After calling out a number, ask them to sit down together to discuss a statement, verse or question. The topics could range from silly to serious. This can be used to discuss one topic, or after a few minutes of discussion, you could ask them to get up and mingle again until you call another number and give them another topic.

GRATITUDE COLLAGES

This activity is an opportunity for group members to encourage one another. It would be especially appropriate as an end-of-the-year (or study) activity or as a closing activity at a retreat. It will take about 60 to 90 minutes to complete, depending on the size of your group.

Materials Needed

❑ Pens or pencils

❑ A small slip of paper for each woman

❑ A box, basket or similar container to hold slips of paper

❑ Several pairs of scissors for cutting paper

❑ A large stack of old magazines

❑ Several bottles of glue or several glue sticks

❑ Several 9x12-inch sheets of colored construction paper, one sheet per woman

Preparation

Lay out the materials on tables around the room.

Procedure

As the women gather, have each one write her name on a slip of paper and put it into a box, basket or other similar container. When the meeting begins, have everyone choose a name from the container. Instruct them that they are to keep the name they chose to themselves. If anyone chooses their own name, tell them to trade it for another.

Have the women cut or tear pictures and words from the magazines that describe the person whose name they picked and then glue the pictures or words to the construction paper provided. **Note:** If anyone is stymied by the name picked because she doesn't know the person at all, she may trade for another name with the help of the leaders. In that situation gathering several of the names to redraw works best.

The women should note the great, wonderful, unique, gifted things about the person as they choose pictures or words from the magazines. The aim is to thank God through illustrative affirmations about the person being depicted.

The activity becomes a guessing game when the whole group is invited to figure out who is being portrayed. Each artist may point out what she was trying to depict about the person.

If visitors are in attendance, the person who brought the visitor may need to trade names with her guest so that her guest is not left out.

HELLO BINGO

This game is a sure way to get the women to mingle as they ask one another questions and gather signatures.

Materials Needed

❏ Photocopies of customized Hello Bingo sheets

❏ Pens or pencils

Preparation

Customize the Bingo sheet to make it appropriate for your group. Choose 16 items, questions, experiences or statements relevant to the women in your group. At the top of each of the squares write various common or wacky questions to ask the participants. The items in the squares may focus on the Bible study topic for that meeting or on work, family, church, faith, sports, fun activities or any other theme. As you put it together, think about what is relevant to the current or recent experiences of the women in your group.

Procedure

Tell the women they are to collect signatures of other group members who fit into each of the Bingo categories. Set a time limit for them to gather signatures—less than 10 minutes is best. When time is up, collect the sheets and have another leader decide the winner. The first to complete the whole sheet or to have the most rows or columns completed is the winner. Rather than a time limit, you could have the first one to complete two rows or columns or the whole sheet shout BINGO!

The following two pages contain a sample Bingo sheet and a blank Bingo sheet for you to copy. The categories at the top of each column are optional.

Option

Assign a category to each of the four columns: e.g., My Favorite Sport, My Worst Color, The Food I Love (or Hate), My Dream Vacation. Then have each woman write her own response in the first square under each category. When they have completed that step, give a time limit, say five to seven minutes, and have them find other group members with the same or similar answers to sign the three squares below each of their own answers.

Sample

HELLO BINGO

Collect one signature for each square. Signatures must include both first and last names.

Leisure Activities	Personal	Likes and Dislikes	Miscellaneous
Doesn't watch TV	Has no siblings	Dislikes sweets	Drives a blue vehicle
Did at least 30 minutes of exercise today	Has the same color of eyes as you	Dislikes sports	Is a native of the community
Played on a school sports team	New to our group in the last month	Likes to eat broccoli	Has been to a foreign country
Plays a musical instrument	Sings in the shower	Dislikes games like this	Has appeared on TV

HELLO BINGO

Collect one signature for each square. Signatures must include both first and last names.

Materials Needed

❑ Five gift certificates from local ice-cream, yogurt or coffee shops

Preparation

Have five women planted in the audience. Each one will have a gift certificate for a local ice-cream, frozen yogurt or coffee shop (or a similar prize).

Procedure

Ask the women to stand, walk around and mingle. When the agreed-upon signal is given, have everyone stop where they are.

Have the first person with a gift certificate shout out "Here I am!" and then give a gift certificate to the person next to him or her. Have the women mingle again and repeat. Do this five times.

INTRODUCTION PROMPTS

Looking for prompts or questions that help women get to know one another beside the tried-and-true "Tell us something about yourself"? Here is a list to get you started.

Personal Information

- Who do you most admire?

- Describe a favorite childhood memory.

- What was your favorite toy?

- What is the best gift you've ever received?

- What was your favorite thing to do as a child?

- How many homes have you lived in? Describe your favorite.

- If you could invent one thing to make housework (or life) easier, what would it be?

- What is your favorite color? How does it affect you?

- Describe your dream vacation (or house or job).

- Where is your favorite place to vacation?

- If you could do anything in the world with no restrictions, what would it be?

- Tell a brief story about something funny that happened to you while on vacation (or growing up or in school or on your wedding day).

- What is the weirdest thing that has ever happened to you?

- Who are you most like: your mother or your father?

- What is one positive thing that you learned from your parents (or mother or father)?

- How many siblings do you have? Where are you in the birth order?

- What did you learn from your siblings? If you have no siblings, what did you learn from your best childhood friend?

- What is your best physical feature (or special talent or ability)?

- Describe the ideal friend.

- Describe your favorite meal.

- What food do you absolutely hate (or love)?

- If you were an animal, what would you be?

- If you had a free day with no responsibilities or restrictions, how would you spend the time?

- What is your favorite candy bar (or vegetable, fruit, restaurant, store, book, etc.)?

- At what store would you love to have unlimited credit?

- Who was your favorite teacher?

- What was your favorite or best subject in school?

- During what time in history would you like to have lived?

The Spiritual Walk

- When do you first remember becoming aware of God?

- Who introduced you to Jesus?

- Where did you first hear the name of Jesus spoken with reverence?

- Who was the first to tell you about the love of Jesus?

- What is your favorite verse (or book of the Bible or biblical character)?

- What is the most difficult thing for you to understand about God?

- What is the most difficult passage in the Bible for you to understand?

- Describe God (or Jesus or the Holy Spirit) in one word (or one sentence).

- What do you find most comforting about God?

- Who is your spiritual hero (besides Jesus)?

- What biblical event would you like to have witnessed?

- With which biblical character would you want to sit down and talk? What would you ask this person?

- What is your favorite hymn or praise song?

- What is God teaching you right now?

- When do you feel closest to the Lord?

- If you could sit down with the Lord, what is one question you would ask Him?

LIONS, MONKEYS, ELEPHANTS

This works best for large groups of 30 or more. It can be a fun way to form discussion groups.

Materials Needed

None, except a room that can be made fairly dark

Procedure

Assign one-third of the women to be lions, one-third to be monkeys and one-third to be elephants.

Explain that the object of this game is for each woman to make her animal sound as loud as she can and find the others in her animal group. The trick is that the women will do this in the dark. Turn out all the lights and tell them to walk around making their sounds and locating the other group members making the same sound. When they find someone making the same sound, they form a group. That group stays together and continues to find more of the same.

After several minutes, turn on the light and have the women sit down with those they have already found. The largest group wins.

Variations

- Use farm animals and their sounds.

- Make up new and unusual sounds.

- Assign things like favorite foods, candy bar names or numbers, and have the women yell out their food/candy/number until they find their groups.

Materials Needed

❑ Name tags

❑ Felt-tip pens

Procedure

Have everyone write their middle names on their name tags rather than their first and/or last names. If some are too embarrassed to do this, ask them to place their middle initial on the tag. Occasionally, someone will have no middle name, so instruct her to give herself one.

Spend the rest of the meeting pointedly using as many middle names as possible. Require the women to refer to each other by middle names. Even have the students use their middle names when talking to you. You can set this up by repeatedly asking them, "What was your name again?"

MINISTRY USING SPECIAL INTERESTS

Special-interest groups—such as a quilting club, a women's choir, a mothers of teens or a fitness group—have strong unity-building effects. The small-group settings can build community as they build bridges to the whole group. They also provide a great way to include new members or even bring in nonbelievers. The Mothers of Preschoolers (MOPS) is a good example of this type of special-interest group. The challenge of learning or working together is also a bonding agent.

Serving others in a learning environment is a great way to incorporate a sense of ministry. Plus, women who don't particularly relate to other areas of ministry often find a home in the women's group through a special-interest group. The ultimate goal of each special-interest group should be to serve others and draw in nonbelievers and newcomers.

The following is a list of possible ideas:

Aerobics Class

Book Club

Community Service Group

Cooking School

Drama Club

Hiking Club

Individual/Team Sports

Nature/Evironmental Club

Needlework/Crafts Class

Puppeteers

Service/Missions Group

Specific Hobbies

Women's Choir

Writing Club

NAME TAG MATCH

Materials Needed

❑ Scissors for cutting paper

❑ Name tags or 3x5-inch index cards

❑ Felt-tip pens

Preparation

Prior to the meeting, cut each name tag into two pieces, making different jagged, curved or zigzag cuts on each one. On the two pieces, write names that can be split into two parts but share similar endings. For example, there are several famous superheroes whose names end in "man," "woman," " boy" or "girl" such as Superman, Wonder Woman, Spider-Man, Batman and Batgirl.

Procedure

As the women gather, have each one select a piece of a name tag. Then give the women two minutes to find the woman who has the matching half—that woman becomes their partner for the meeting.

Variations

- Use famous people who share the same last names or use famous pairs. You can get names from collections of biographies.

- Before cutting the cards or tags apart, write a different Scripture passage on each card—or the verse on one half and the reference on the other half—then have each woman find the woman who has her match. This would be a great way to review Scripture memory verses.

ROLL SHARING

Materials Needed

❑ A roll or two of toilet paper (depending on the size of the group)

Procedure

Have the women form a circle, either standing or sitting. Pass around a roll of toilet paper instructing them to take any number of pieces of toilet paper, up to 10 pieces. Give no further instructions until after the roll has made it around the circle.

After everyone has their sheets of toilet paper, announce that for every sheet of toilet paper each group member has selected, she must share something about herself that other group members don't know. As each person shares one thing, she rips off one piece of toilet paper and throws it into the center. This activity works best if each person shares only one piece of information at a time, giving them a chance to build on the others' ideas and stories.

Variation

You could substitute pieces of candy or other small items, but allow them to keep the items.

SEVEN ANSWERS

This community-building activity gathers women to share responses to seven questions. Then, with the whole group, they share a few more details of why they answered as they did. The topics can be customized to your particular group.

Materials Needed

❑ Felt-tip pen

❑ Seven 8½x11-inch pieces of paper

❑ Tape

❑ Photocopies of the questions you develop

❑ Pens or pencils

Preparation

Prepare the room for this activity by writing the numerals 1 through 7 on separate 8½x11-inch pieces of paper and taping them to the walls around the room. These numerals indicate the seven stations that will correspond with the answers of each question. Prepare a sheet with a set of seven questions with seven answers for each question. These questions can be lead-ins for the meeting theme. Make photocopies of the question sheets, one for each woman attending.

Procedure

As the women gather, give each one a sheet of questions and a pen or pencil. Explain that they are to answer the questions quietly without talking to anyone else. Don't tell them about the numbers on the wall. Give them a few minutes to answer each of the seven questions.

After they have completed the questions, ask all of the students who answered the first question with answer 1 to walk over and stand under the numeral 1, so on through answer 7. Once at the stations, instruct each one of them to briefly share with the whole group why they answered as they did. Follow this same procedure with the rest of the questions and answers.

Sample Question

Circle the person who most supported you as you were growing up.

1. Your mom

2. Your dad

3. Your grandmother

4. Your grandfather

5. A sibling

6. A neighbor

7. A friend

Questions can be about anything: hobbies, politics, Bible characters, pets, dream vacations, etc. They can be serious or trivial. They can also relate to a study topic. What is important is that the questions bring the group to a new level of sharing and understanding, giving them new topics of common interest with one another.

SMALL-GROUP QUESTIONS

Choose a Scripture verse, a news item, a quote or any single topic question. Place the women in small groups of four to six women each to discuss it. This could be done in place of a warm-up activity or a meeting opening by immediately assigning women to small groups as they walk into the room. It is a good alternative to letting them gather and chat only with their group of friends. Have the groups discuss for about 10 minutes; then begin the meeting or activity.

YOUR EULOGY

This activity takes about 2 minutes to introduce, 5 minutes for each participant to complete and about 10 minutes (depending on group size) to share eulogies. This would be a great closing activity for a retreat or at the end of a study on self-worth.

Materials Needed

❑ Pens or pencils

❑ Paper

Procedure

Begin by asking: **How do you want to be remembered? Strangely enough, people who have achieved great deeds in life often reflect that their accomplishments don't fully express who they really are inside—only what they have done.**

Eulogies summarize the person's life by sharing characteristics of and memories about the person. What could be said about your life thus far? What do you believe and stand for? What is important to you? This is your chance to tell us who you really are by writing your own eulogy. Be honest and open and don't hold back. This isn't boasting—it's honestly evaluating how you see yourself and who you are on the inside.

Distribute pens or pencils and paper. Give the women a few minutes to write a short eulogy. Allow time for each woman to share her eulogy.

Variation

Have the women write inscriptions for their tombstones. Ask: **If you lived your life the way you would like to, how would you like to be remembered by those whose lives you touched? What would you like to have inscribed on your tombstone?**

Give the women a few minutes to write their inscriptions; then have a time of group sharing.

New from Focus on the Family®

The Women's Ministry That Has It All!

Kit includes

- *The Focus on the Family Women's Ministry Guide*
- *Crafts and Activities for Women's Ministry*
- *Women of Worth* Bible Study
- *Healing the Heart* Bible Study
- *Balanced Living* Bible Study
- *The Blessings of Friendships* Bible Study

Focus on the Family Women's Series Kit
Group Starter Kit • Bible Study
ISBN 08307.33574

Research shows that women are the backbone of Christian congregations in America,* but many are overwhelmed and in need of a break to reconnect with the Lord. Focus on the Family has **combined the best features of women's ministries**—Bible studies, prayer, fellowship, Scripture memory and activities— and created **new resources for women of all ages** so that they can *relax* and *reflect* on God.

By learning to define themselves based on God's Word, women will decrease their feelings of being inadequate and overwhelmed, and increase their sense of self-worth while joining in fellowship with God and other Christian women. Help women come together with the new ministry that has it all!

The Focus on the Family Women's Series
is available where Christian books are sold.

Gospel Light

*From Barna Research, *Women Are the Backbone of the Christian Congregations in America,* March 6, 2000.

We've Combined the Best of Women's Ministry for One Comprehensive Experience!

These resources provide a multitude of ideas for giving women the much-desired opportunity to get together and share different life experiences—joys and sorrows—to build deep, Christ-centered relationships.

Women of Worth Bible Study

Women often define themselves by what others expect of them. Many feel they come up short when they try to have it all—beauty, family, career, success. This study helps women find their true identity and purpose through their relationship with Christ. Includes topics such as defining worth, body image, femininity, sexuality and relationships.
ISBN 08307.33361

Healing the Heart Bible Study

This study helps women experience emotional and spiritual healing by understanding the hurts and pain in their lives and finding restoration through Christ. Topics include recognizing the effects of sin, mending your thoughts, forgiveness and letting go of the past.
ISBN 08307.33620

Balanced Living Bible Study

When women strive to do it all, they end up feeling stressed out, fatigued and disconnected from God. This study gives women the tools to balance the various demands on their time while maintaining an intimate relationship with God. Topics include why women overextend themselves, separating the important from the urgent and managing the pressures of life.
ISBN 08307.33639

The Blessings of Friendships Bible Study

In today's fast-paced, busy world it's difficult for women to establish and maintain strong, healthy relationships. In this study, women will explore the nature of relationships and Christ's model for them. Some of the topics covered include forgiveness, being honest and vulnerable, the fine art of listening, receiving correction and the blessings of community.
ISBN 08307.33647

The Focus on the Family Women's Ministry Guide

This comprehensive guide gives leaders everything they need to set up and run an effective ministry for women of all ages and life situations.
ISBN 08307.33388

Crafts and Activities for Women's Ministry

This book is packed with ideas for adding fun and creativity to women's ministry meetings and special events. Includes reproducible craft patterns, activities and more!
ISBN 08307.33671

The Focus on the Family Women's Series
is available where Christian books are sold.

Gospel Light

STRENGTHEN MARRIAGES.
STRENGTHEN YOUR CHURCH.

Here's Everything You Need for a Dynamic Marriage Ministry!

Group Starter Kit includes

• Nine Bible Studies: *The Masterpiece Marriage*, *The Passionate Marriage*, *The Fighting Marriage*, *The Model Marriage*, *The Surprising Marriage*, *The Giving Marriage*, *The Covenant Marriage*, *The Abundant Marriage* and *The Blended Marriage*

• *The Focus on the Family Marriage Ministry Guide*

• *An Introduction to the Focus on the Family Marriage Series* video

Focus on the Family ®
Marriage Series
Group Starter Kit
Kit Box
Bible Study/Marriage
ISBN 08307.32365

The overall health of your church is directly linked to the health of its marriages. And in light of today's volatile pressures and changing lifestyles, your commitment to nurture and strengthen marriages needs tangible, practical help. Now **Focus on the Family—the acknowledged leader in Christian marriage and family resources**—gives churches a comprehensive group study series dedicated to enriching marriages. Strengthen marriages and strengthen your church with **The Focus on the Family Marriage Series**.

The Focus on the Family Marriage Series
is available where Christian books are sold.

Gospel Light

Welcome to the Family!

As you participate in the *Focus on the Family Women's Series*, it is our prayerful hope that God will deepen your understanding of His plan for you and that He will strengthen the women relationships in your congregation and community.

This series is just one of the many helpful, insightful, and encouraging resources produced by Focus on the Family. In fact, that's what Focus on the Family is all about—providing inspiration, information, and biblically based advice to people in all stages of life.

It began in 1977 with the vision of one man, Dr. James Dobson, a licensed psychologist and author of 18 best-selling books on marriage, parenting, and family. Alarmed by the societal, political, and economic pressures that were threatening the existence of the American family, Dr. Dobson founded Focus on the Family with one employee and a once-a-week radio broadcast aired on only 36 stations.

Now an international organization, the ministry is dedicated to preserving Judeo-Christian values and strengthening and encouraging families through the life-changing message of Jesus Christ. Focus ministries reach families worldwide through 10 separate radio broadcasts, two television news features, 13 publications, 18 Web sites, and a steady series of books and award-winning films and videos for people of all ages and interests.

We'd love to hear from you!